ONE

Conversations on Life, Death, and Music

LAST

MIKE AYERS

SONG

Illustrations by Studio Muti

ABRAMS IMAGE, NEW YORK

CONTENTS

FOREWORD
BY JIM JAMES

LIFE IS SOMETIMES SO VERY BEAUTIFUL. YOU just can't *believe* how beautiful it all is!!! And so many days I feel so lucky and I am so glad to be alive, with the breeze in my hair and the sun on my face. Laughing with a friend . . . glowing in a lover's touch. Knowing that someone truly loves me and sees me for who I really am. Family. Listening to or making beautiful music. Those things that make it feel so great to be human and *alive*.

I'm not frightened of dying. In fact, there have been so many times in my life that I wished I were dead. There have been times I felt so much physical or mental pain . . . I felt so alone and lost that I just wished that it would all end, or that if some magic doorway suddenly appeared in the middle of the street I just happened to be walking down . . . and I looked through it and saw another world . . . I would just go ahead and walk through . . . see if it was any easier over there in that other world, 'cause god damn, it is fucking tough down here sometimes.

Don't get me wrong, I don't want to die. There are so many things I still wish to experience, if I am lucky enough to get to do so. Having a child. Making more music. Making more love. Making more laughs. How many more times? How much longer will I get? Can I keep it together?

There were times when I felt so alone and so desperate that I thought, *Fuck it.* But I never had the motivation, when it came right down to it, to actually literally leave this world.

That's when I knew that what I was feeling, as terrible as it may have been, was not nearly as strong as what some of my loved ones must have been feeling when they *really* said fuck it and literally left this world. I wonder what song was their last and if they knew that it was at the time?

I have written songs about several of those people. Some of those songs the dead sang to me in my dreams, and I awoke knowing they wanted this world to hear them.

I have had many close friends and acquaintances die "before their time." Either by their own hand or by the hand of fate or the universe or whatever you want to call it—I have seen a lot of young people die. And of course, each time I think—it could have been me.

But then I always think of my father's words—that when it's your time to go, it's your time to go; there's nothing you can do about it. He loves to say this. It brings me great comfort. So I don't worry about it too much.

I think this question about the last song you'd want to hear is a very interesting one, as it shows us how much we all have in common on this subject of death. No matter what label the world tries to put on a person, or what belief system one does or does not ascribe to—we can all find some common ground in death . . . and we should be using that to find more common ground in life.

Although all the musicians in this book have completely different answers, there is a through line of beauty and creativity when thinking about death that we all share, because, in this beautiful way, death itself is our final act of creation. Every aspect of it—how one dies, when one dies, what type of ceremony one does or does not want, how one wishes to be buried or not buried or set afire at sea in a Viking funeral, their ashes then collected and scattered around a hard-to-find tombstone in the middle of a forest with only the single word "weird" carved upon its face (that's

9

mine) . . . There is something so creative and artistic about death. Even in the most seemingly "routine and normal" deaths, there is such beauty and mystery. I will never forget watching my grandfather die after having lived a good long life, surrounded by his family at ninety years old, taking his final breaths, all of us thinking each breath was the last, until . . . finally . . . it was. And after that final death rattle his body turned from "human" into something more like a tree or stone, meant to return to nature right before our eyes, to become a life source from which some new being will begin again. So natural and mysterious and surreal and completely normal and circular, like the moon or the sun or the earth itself, we go round and round . . . as we end this round to begin the next in some way we will never be able to fully understand. I am quite certain this book will provide inspiration not only in the way you think about your final wishes, but in the way you view your everyday life and creativity, with all its small births and deaths.

Music is such a special thing because it never dies. A song is this eternal vessel that, once born, can never be killed. I think about all the dramatic scenarios, like all the power being wiped out, or all the instruments being gathered and smashed up— that'd be okay! We could still sing! And even if singing were not permitted, we would still sing inside our hearts and minds. Even if there were no humans . . . songs are spirits that float on the breeze, drifting from this world to that, sung by every creature imaginable in familiar tunes and keys and those we cannot even begin to imagine in scale and structure so bizarre.

Because of recording technology or concert set lengths, we tend to put time limits on music . . . but music has no real duration. There is no beginning or end; you could have any song forever, and you could sing it a million different ways. Songs drift down into our souls from space and other dimensions and float up into our hearts from the earth beneath our feet. What could be more natural than music? Music is God. God is love. Love never dies.

WHAT'S THE
LAST SONG
YOU'D EVER
WANT
TO HEAR?

HOW DO I WANT TO DIE? I BET YOU'VE asked yourself that hundreds, thousands, maybe even millions of times over the course of your life. I ask it of myself all the time. All. The. Time. Why do we do this? Why are we obsessed with death?

Is it simply because it's so unknown and that's super scary and we as human beings are not content with living and breathing until we know everything? Think about it. For thousands of years, human beings were just existing on earth, eating things, having sex with each other, killing one another—basically the plot of *Game of Thrones*, forever. But while we humans have been running around doing these things, a constant hovering over us was the moon. The moon was up above, just hanging out, doing its gravitational-pull thing to make waves in the ocean . . . but honestly, not much else. But then humans at some point decided, hey, they wanted to go to the moon. Fly into *outer space*, land on it, and plant a flag. They weren't content to just let it be. Humans were basically like, *Wow, that moon is just hanging out, and, well . . . fuck that. We'll show it who's boss.*

Conquering the moon is something humans never thought was possible, but then it became possible. And with that, the mystery was erased. The moon, as a rock floating around the earth, became pretty mainstream. People found out what its deal was. And it stopped being considered part of the *unknown*. I bet people before the last century talked about the moon all the time. All the time! Because they had no idea really what it was. And that was its allure.

However, the mystery of death remains intact. I'm sorry, but we're not going to have a definitive answer on what happens when you die . . . ever. Maybe heaven. Maybe hell. Maybe something else. Maybe nothing. Nobody truly knows. It's just speculation and faith and it will remain that way for *eternity*.

That's why we're obsessed with death. Or at least I am. The stakes are so high. It's so final, that moment when you're slipping into darkness or light or whatever (we don't know!).

So because of all this, I truly believe that the last song you'd pick to hear while on earth is a window into your soul, into your essence, into everything that might or might not encapsulate your time here. It's a connection that's deep and profound, something that speaks volumes about you, or to you, either through the melody or the words or the first time you heard it or all of the above.

This book explores how thirty-two musicians arrived at their own answers to this question. But before we get to that, here's a little look into how I got the answers contained within. Most people want to know the parameters of the scenario when they're picking their last song. This is how I suggested they think about it.

FOR THIS EXERCISE, HOW WILL I DIE? DO I GET TO PICK?

You get to pick! It's really up to you. If you want to die in a plane crash—well, that sucks, but, okay, what would be the last song you'd want to hear as you're going down? If you want to just die in bed due to old age, that's cool, too. The big thing here is to think about death more as the abstract concept and what you'd want to pair with it. Like, death is french fries—it could be thin cut, steak fries, delicious Five Guys fries, which are cooked in peanut oil and thus godly—whatever. You don't know what you're getting. But fries are coming. So what is the only thing you want to dip those fries into?

DOES THE SONG HAVE TO HAVE SOME DEEP MEANING FOR ME?

I mean, it doesn't have to. But ideally it does. Because why else would this be the last recorded sounds you'd choose to hear?

Think about the big moments in our lives that have a song to accompany them: Birthdays. First dance at middle school. First time you did it. First dance at your wedding. New Year's Eve. Graduation. The songs that soundtracked these moments have attached themselves to you, they've come to represent something for you. So you should at least consider something that has stayed with you. But there's nothing wrong with frivolity, either.

SHOULD THERE BE LYRICS?

Again, up to you—it really depends on how you feel about those words. Do you find them soothing? Do they say something that you've always connected to? Do they say something that sums up life or the afterlife? Is the singer's voice comforting? For me, I've never been that keen on metal. So I wouldn't want anything screamy. But metal fans would probably adore some screamy as they die. The human voice is something we attach ourselves to, and a musician's voice, in particular, is something we love, when we think about the bands or acts or singers we adore. So you should absolutely pick something with words. But also, maybe don't? Some of the most beautiful pieces of music ever written were devoid of words. Words can be distracting. Words make our minds active. And if we're slowing down, getting ready to

exit, do we really want to be focusing on language and meaning? It's tough.

HEY, CAN IT BE, LIKE, A WHOLE ALBUM?

Hey, no. Albums are super long! This isn't some desert-island-disc thing, where you get to take ten albums or whatever to some amazing private island and live *Cast Away*–style, with a bunch of sick records, and then die. The idea of listening to an album before you die is an interesting one, and yes, that would likely be a hard choice. But a single song is a compact moment in time. It's where the stakes are highest. You're visualizing your last couple minutes and there's no turning back. So that's a big reason why we're just sticking to the song concept. Sorry. Trust me. One song says more about you than one album.

DO YOU MEAN IF I DIED TODAY OR IN FIFTY OR SIXTY YEARS, WHEN I'M OLD, GRAY, AND VERY KNOWLEDGEABLE ABOUT SOUP?

Yeah, this is where it gets a bit abstract. When I asked this question to the artists in this book, often this would be the first question they'd ask me back. Because it's hard to say, "Hey, this is the song I want to hear in fifty or sixty years when I'm old and gray and a huge fan of soup." How do you know? What if your song tastes change? What if you wake up one morning when you're fifty and realize, "Wow, that last song I chose, which has been 'The Humpty Dance' by Digital Underground—I don't think I like it anymore." Sure, it's hard to say that what you like now is something you'd like in ten, twenty, or fifty years. But is there a song or a piece of music that hasn't left you, even though you've changed? That's critical. If you can identify a song that you're still attached to, as you've left certain parts of your life and entered new ones—and it's remained a constant fixture, a constant source of pleasure or comfort or both—that's a strong candidate. Because you change. The recording doesn't. It never will. It's a moment that artist captured in time.

A BIT MORE ABOUT
THE EMOTIONAL
CONNECTION THING

We're all connected to music through our emotions. Sometimes the emotions can be very, very intense. I have vivid memories of *crying* through U2's *Achtung Baby* in high school. Hormones were raging and girls were breaking my heart on a monthly basis. I had spectacular bouts of acne; so much so, I had to take prescription drugs. It sucked hard. Bono and the Edge and Larry Mullen Jr.

and Adam Clayton were there for me. I think there was one night, I'm not joking, where I listened to the song "So Cruel" ten times in a row. *Ten times.* That's insane to me at this point. But back then, it wasn't. I was confused and sad and definitely depressed and didn't understand why I was becoming the poster child for rejection—and somehow that song allowed me to cope. To exhale. To find a way to keep moving. It's weird to say, but everything about it—the tempo, the melody, Bono's phrasing in the lyrics—combined into this five-minute-and-forty-nine-second song that worked perfectly with my emotional state and being. It's strange that music can do this to a person. And that we let it. We let it make sense of and explain the world to us in ways that nothing else can.

THINK ABOUT
YOUR LAST MOMENTS

So what do you want your last moments to remind you of? Or better yet, what do you want to be surrounded by in your last moments? I think it's safe to say that we all want to go in peace, perhaps with loved ones by our sides. We don't want to go in a shark attack and we don't want to have fear or terror or the sudden sinking feeling that we've wasted our lives and there's no turning back.

So what should those last moments evoke? And what sounds and words would evoke them? Is there a song that would sum up your most important, intense relationship with another person? Or yourself?

I've had what I characterize as two near-death experiences in my life. One, when I was in fourth grade and it had snowed, forcing school to close for the day. Behind my house there was a wooded area, with a slope that allowed for sledding—but only if you stayed on a certain path. My younger sister had veered off the path and I chased her, high-stepping through snow mounds; I tripped and fell on a stick that punctured my neck, about an inch away from my Adam's apple, windpipe, and jugular vein. I ran up to the house, with the stick *still hanging out of my neck*. I had to get stitches, and there's still a scar there today.

The other time, I was in a parking lot with my dad. I was in my early twenties and we were going to dinner. A brutal rainstorm had just terrorized the area and there was some residual thunder lingering about. We started to get out of the car and we heard this unfathomably loud crack. About five feet from us, lightning hit the ground. Yes, I know that you can get struck by lightning and not die, but I'm sorry—if highly charged electrical bolts are coming down *from the sky* and hitting me, I'm dead. There's no recovery. There's no superpowers that magically transfer to my body. That's it. Done.

Now that I think about it, weather seems like it's out to get me.

But anyway.

For me, those were moments devoid of sound. The woods were quiet after the snowfall; the only sound that permeated that moment was the loud wail I let out after being stabbed by the forest itself. And the post-rainstorm lightning crack was also devoid of sound, except for the *POP*, but I'm fairly certain we had just been listening to Hootie and the Blowfish. It was the late nineties and Hootie was hot. You couldn't go anywhere without hearing Hootie. My dad loved Hootie. The radio loved Hootie. Now that I think about it, the girl who inspired me to listen to "So Cruel" ten times in a row *loved Hootie*.

I think that a lot of death occurs in this fashion. There's no choice for our last moments. It could be today or tomorrow. It could be in seventy years. And for me, finding that connection to a song that evokes a final moment can define so much for us right now, while we're still here.

COLIN MELOY

THE DECEMBERISTS

———

LAST SONG

"Astral Weeks"

BY VAN MORRISON (1968)

V AN MORRISON WAS "BROWN EYED Girl" to me. It was my parents. It was hippie music. It was the Baby Boomers. I was into new wave and punk rock and stuff. But for my last song, I think it would be "Astral Weeks." I was only introduced to it in my late teens or early twenties, by the Waterboys—they do a cover of "Sweet Thing" from the *Astral Weeks* album on *Fisherman's Blues*. I have connected with music in a real strong, visceral way, in my thirties and now forties. But nothing really compares to the spell that a record or a song or an artist can have over you when you're sixteen, seventeen, and in your twenties.

COLIN MELOY

Colin Meloy is the frontman for literary folk-rock band the Decemberists and a *New York Times* bestselling children's author. The Decemberists have released eight albums in their twenty-year career, with the last three landing in the top ten of the Billboard 200; 2010's *The King Is Dead* hit number one.

"Astral Weeks" itself is an incredible piece of music. This feel of continuity is so much of the piece. It's not intellectualized. I don't mean the way it appears, but when you listen to it, it feels very stream of consciousness—but also it was recorded very quickly and spontaneously. It feels like the unvarnished vision of an artist.

So why would I want to listen to it as the last song before I died? For one thing, it's a great song. It is also the first piece of music that both of my kids heard. When Hank, my eldest son, was born, there was some discussion. We were in the hospital, and I think we had brought a little speaker along with us, because we knew we were going to be in there for a few days. And we were in the days after you've had a kid, where the baby is sleeping and waking, sleeping and waking—and all of a sudden you have walked through doors that you can never go out of. You're in this momentary divide: on one side, you are childless; on the other side, you're a parent. So you're in that weird headspace, a fog, where everything is new. You're in the presence of someone for whom everything is new. Nothing is familiar. Everything becomes weighted with importance. There was a brief discussion about how, if we put on some music, it will be the first music that the baby hears. What is that going to be? I think my wife and I quickly decided that "Astral Weeks" was the thing that would be the first piece of music.

It's organic. It's nothing that Hank remembers, and I can't even imagine what your consciousness is like when it's your first time breathing outside the womb. It was as much for us as it was for him. And it was also an opportunity to put ourselves in that mind-set, like, *What is it to hear music for the first time?*

When our second kid was born, we were prepared. We were at the hospital, with the speaker, with the phone, and we were both like, "It should just be 'Astral Weeks.'" So both of them, their first piece of music, first melodic sounds, was "Astral Weeks." When I reflect on the last bit of music that I'd want to hear, I think "Astral Weeks" is that as well. I think it is appropriate for the first and last.

Van was a big improviser. "Astral Weeks" is like three chords, the main verse part of it. When I write, I lock in and melody is super important. I don't know that he writes his melodies each time. I think it's very free-flowing, particularly in the early days. The funny thing is, he totally disavowed what he had done with the album *Astral Weeks* and thought it was an uncommercial mess. He just wanted to make money and made *Moondance* next. They were only separated by a year, but sound so different. They were coming from a different mind, a different artist. But it was him just deciding he needed to make something commercial. And he did.

Death is very common in the Decemberists' songs. It's as common as it comes. The songs that don't touch on death are in the minority at this point. There's lots of dying. Drowning, murder, and also just dying.

What "Astral Weeks" is about, what that means, I guess, is up for interpretation from anybody. It's "astral"—connected to the stars, which are infinite—but just for "weeks," a known, definitive amount of time. That reminds me of childbirth or the experience of having a kid, like what it takes to be a parent. It's the moment of being equally in love and feeling unmoored. I think weeks spent in that way are "astral" in how they present themselves.

So stepping over into death is one of those crossings through doors that you'll never return from. Venturing into the slipstream. That song could very well be about death, as much as it is about whatever Van Morrison was thinking about in 1968.

"Astral Weeks"

ARTIST
Van Morrison

ALBUM
Astral Weeks

LENGTH
7 minutes, 6 seconds

RECORDED
In one take on September 25, 1968

IS THIS SONG ABOUT DEATH?
You be the judge. Morrison at one point reportedly said that the song is "Like transforming energy, or going from one source to another with it being born again like a rebirth. I remember reading about you having to die to be born. It's one of those songs where you can see the light at the end of the tunnel and that's basically what the song says."

LAUREN MAYBERRY

CHVRCHES

LAST SONG

"Firework"

BY KATY PERRY (2010)

I BATTED AROUND SO MANY DIFFERENT ideas of something I'd want in my last moment. I tried to choose songs that were more stoic, or what I imagined the mood would be when you're going through something like that. Or trying to find more arty ones or ones that seemed more profound. But when I was thinking about it, would I really want to listen to something profound or depressing in that moment? Probably not. So then I went on a completely different tangent: Do I want to listen to something that reminds me of my parents? Being a kid and growing up? In that moment *what do you really want?*

I settled on a song that would remind me of nice times I had in life with friends and loved ones. But it's not heavy. It's not emotionally heavy. It's warm, it's nostalgic, but it's not "Hurt" by Johnny Cash.

It's "Firework" by Katy Perry. Don't laugh. If you're in that moment, and you're on your deathbed, what do you want? I've always had good times with Katy Perry, and she always puts her money where her mouth is about what kind of person she wants to be. So I'd like to be reminded of that. Also, I really love the message of that song. There's a reason why that song connects with a lot of people. I used to be snobby about pop music, but there's some really good, emotional pop music. I put "Firework" in that category.

In hindsight, I was obsessed with pop music until I was like sixteen or seventeen. Then you learn about other things, other art forms. I think that is valid, but I think what I was doing was really that *High Fidelity* thing, where it's that "What you like, not what you are like" thing. You don't really know anything about yourself, so you're manifesting, you're projecting. There's always been shit pop music, but there's always been great pop music as well.

What do we want when we die? I think I want something that feels like a warm, cozy blanket. And I've definitely drunk-cried in the clubs to "Firework." Not because I was sad, but because I was moved by the emotion of the song. What a lovely message! I remember one time I was standing next to this dad who had brought his daughter to this Katy show and they both were singing along, they both knew all the words. I think there's something in that, if you can connect with something in that way.

So much of life is quite lonely or you're just trying to connect to people, figure people out. Move through life's obstacles. Feel like you know somebody, feel like you're understood. In those moments, something as simple as a three-and-a-half-minute pop song can connect so many people who are so completely different, who are insane, and awful, and wonderful in their own ways—but those are the things that bring us together. We all have this emotional debt. That song pushes my buttons.

I used to run this women's collective in Scotland and we wanted to start a club night where we picked female artists, because there wasn't really anything like that in Glasgow. I had been playing in bands since I was a teenager, and 99 percent of the time, I was the only female in the lineup. We were like, "Let's start a club night!" And then it became a magazine, and a radio show, and a website. Everyone was working full-time jobs; I was in a band and working a full-time job, and trying to do this club thing. Some of my fondest memories of that time were when it was almost 3:00 a.m., the club night was almost done, and everybody was allowed to have a couple of beers and sing along to Katy Perry.

It was quite a transitional period for the band and for me to figure out how to exist as a woman in public. There was a lot going on and everybody else was male or managed by men—but when you're getting rape threats, there's only so much they can understand about what that's like. I feel like "Firework" exemplified how important female friendships were then and still are.

We heard it in the back of a taxi the other day and were like, "This song is just so classic." It didn't necessarily feel of its time in terms of the production. It's almost like Eurovision-meets-ABBA in the arrangement; the melody is just so classic. That's what will make it last, like a Cher song or a Cyndi Lauper song. In the band we always talk about "dance cries" being a genre we want to corner. You can dance to it, you can cry to it, or you can do both at the same time. "Firework" is our blueprint.

I really admire Katy Perry's fearlessness. Every iteration of Katy Perry, I've always believed it. I believed when she

"Firework"

ARTIST
Katy Perry

ALBUM
Teenage Dream

LENGTH
3 minutes, 48 seconds

CHART POSITION
No. 1 on the Billboard Hot 100 on December 18, 2010. It was there for an impressive four weeks.

IS KATY PERRY'S "FIREWORK" ABOUT DEATH? A MINIATURE INVESTIGATION
Perry said this to MTV News in 2010: "I really believe in people and I believe people have a spark to be a firework. A lot of times it's only us that's standing in the way of reaching our goals, fulfilling our destinies, being the best version of who we possibly can be."

And the music video certainly espouses that. There are sparks! (Literally coming out of Katy Perry.) But there are also sparks coming out of everyday young people who are struggling with all the issues young people struggle with. Depression. Feelings of isolation. Feelings of not being good enough. Too fat. Too weird. Too close to death and no longer wanting to live. There's one tween girl who is wrestling with cancer. She's bald from the chemo treatments, so it's clear the end could be near. Or maybe not. But "Firework" is the catalyst that gets her out of bed, back into the world. Maybe that's not directly about death—it's more of a middle finger to death—but it's still a narration on it. Katy Perry may have written a song about fulfilling our destinies, and for one of the video's stars, that destiny is to keep living. Which is the direct opposite of death. But you can't say it's about life when you have that dichotomy. Right?

LAUREN MAYBERRY

LAUREN MAYBERRY

Lauren Mayberry is the lead singer of Scottish electro-pop band CHVRCHES. Formed in 2011, the band has released three albums and headlined major concert venues around the world, such as Radio City Music Hall, the Greek Theater, and the Alexandra Palace in London

was running around in a cupcake that that was her idea. That was her vision. But I also believed when she changed. That's what the real Katy Perry wants to do.

Whenever people have the "role model" conversation, I think it's a bit of a double-edged sword. Yes, she has a lot of young fans, but she's also a grown woman. That's why when you go to a Katy Perry show, you see a lot of little girls, but also women my age. She's a grown lady that's in charge of her own agency, her own body. I like that her essence is tongue-in-cheek and camp; that there are jokes for the grown-ups. But at the end of the day, the message is very positive for young girls. Yeah, she's running around in emoji poo, but that's fun—pop music is supposed to be fun. And then when it comes to serious moments, she's encouraging people to be conscious, to be kind. Be themselves. I feel like there's so much rhetoric in the world, for young women especially, to not be that. And the fact that she's putting on costumes, it's to tell a story. To be a character. It's not to be cute or pretty or desirable to men. It's telling a story and being silly. I think that is sadly beaten out of women a lot. So, I'm like, "Katy for president."

A. C. NEWMAN

THE NEW PORNOGRAPHERS

———

LAST SONG

"*Baker Street*"

BY GERRY RAFFERTY (1978)

I'M NOT SURE I'D WANT TO HAVE A FINAL song. That feels like a last meal or something. It feels like a horrific event. Like, prepare to hear your last song, *ever*. Nobody wants to die.

So I don't want there to be a real answer to this. That said, I think I would go with "Baker Street" by Gerry Rafferty. There's something about it that's bittersweet, yet triumphant. To me, it's the most perfectly recorded song. And there's something about the message in it that I really relate to.

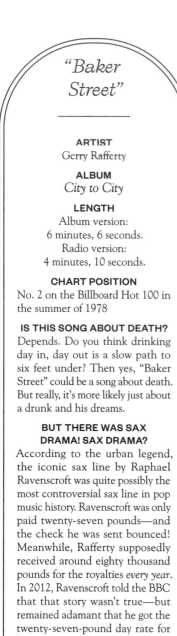

"Baker Street"

ARTIST
Gerry Rafferty

ALBUM
City to City

LENGTH
Album version:
6 minutes, 6 seconds.
Radio version:
4 minutes, 10 seconds.

CHART POSITION
No. 2 on the Billboard Hot 100 in
the summer of 1978

IS THIS SONG ABOUT DEATH?
Depends. Do you think drinking
day in, day out is a slow path to
six feet under? Then yes, "Baker
Street" could be a song about death.
But really, it's more likely just about
a drunk and his dreams.

**BUT THERE WAS SAX
DRAMA! SAX DRAMA?**
According to the urban legend,
the iconic sax line by Raphael
Ravenscroft was quite possibly the
most controversial sax line in pop
music history. Ravenscroft was only
paid twenty-seven pounds—and
the check he was sent bounced!
Meanwhile, Rafferty supposedly
received around eighty thousand
pounds for the royalties *every year*.
In 2012, Ravenscroft told the BBC
that that story wasn't true—but
remained adamant that he got the
twenty-seven-pound day rate for
his work.

The final line is "You're going home." That seems like a good exit line. I remember when it was a hit, when I was a kid. I really liked it. You just listen to a song in a very superficial way when you're a kid. You just think, "This song's cool, I like this." And then, as you get older, you start listening to the words and realize: "Oh, this song is . . . There's more to this song." Lines like "You used to think that it was so easy / But you're trying, you're trying now."

There are so many songs that I'd list as my all-time favorite song. So many of them come from that same general time, like Joni Mitchell's "Free Man in Paris," Queen and David Bowie's "Under Pressure," or "Baker Street." Obviously, those songs are amazing. But there's something about the way I heard them when I was a child that stuck with me. They sounded like magic.

I think "Baker Street" has a few combinations of things. It tapped into something I liked as a kid, lyrically. But also later in life, too. Near the end of the song, he sings, "He's got this dream about buying some land / He's gonna give up the booze and the one-night stands / And then he'll settle down / In some quiet town / And forget about everything." I moved to Woodstock, and I remember that feeling. I still feel that way. Wanting to just get away. Wanting to have this quiet place that's yours. But then, at the end of the song, he basically says, "But you're never going to do that." That's the point of the song where I'm like, "Wait, you are! You are going to do that." You're not a rolling stone. But I guess in this case, I'm dying, I am going home.

When people listen to my music, there's a cognitive dissonance. They think my music sounds like it should be happy, but it isn't. When people listen to a song that is upbeat, but the lyrics are fairly dark, they'd rather think it's gibberish than think I was writing something very dark. The New Pornographers' song "Whiteout Conditions" is

A. C. NEWMAN

A. C. NEWMAN

A. C. Newman is the frontman for beloved power-pop rock band the New Pornographers, a group that has featured an eclectic cast of musicians over the years, including Dan Bejar of Destroyer and Neko Case. A.C. has released several albums under his own name and has also composed film scores.

basically a song about dealing with depression, even though it's an upbeat pop song. There's a little bridge section that says, "The sky will come for you once / Just sit tight until it's done." That's basically saying, "You'll die eventually, just hang out till then."

Gerry Rafferty was in such an in-between state. His band Stealers Wheel was over and he was trying to figure out what to do next. He didn't know that all the music he'd be known for was yet to come. He didn't know he was going to have a song that was much more iconic than "Stuck in the Middle with You." I like that vibe. It's a sense of "What am I doing here?"

The production on "Baker Street" is so layered—it's almost psychedelic music, but it's late seventies psychedelic music. And talk about life stages. That song has various stages! It opens with that psychedelic guitar part, moves into the epic saxophone riff that everybody knows, then settles into this very cool, mellow verse. And it's got one of my favorite guitar solos. It's so effective, so simple. I love when people go from solo into solo.

I've never played "Baker Street." It's always been a dream of mine—but I know we would fail.

KILLER MIKE

———

LAST SONG

"Untitled"

BY KILLER MIKE (2012)

I WROTE A SONG CALLED "UNTITLED" years ago. This is the first time that I've said I "wrote" it. The song more came through me. It talked about my fears, my passions, my submissions, in the most honest way. It's abstract and surreal, but it gets to the point immediately when I say, "It takes a woman's womb to make a Christ or Dalai Lama / The world might take that child, turn that child into a monster / The Lord'll take a monster and fashion him a saint / I present you Malcolm X for those who saying that He can't / Saying that He won't, when I know He will / You usually don't know it's you until you getting killed / For real."

"Untitled"

ARTIST
Killer Mike

ALBUM
R.A.P. Music

LENGTH
3 minutes, 54 seconds

RELEASED
March 16, 2012

IS THIS SONG ABOUT DEATH?
Most definitely. He literally says, "I'm only going once." And the video depicts Killer Mike's head being served on a platter!

KILLER MIKE

Killer Mike is an Atlanta-based rapper who does it all: releases solo albums, records and tours with EL-P as the acclaimed duo Run the Jewels, created the Netflix series *Trigger Warning with Killer Mike*, and has collaborated with numerous other musicians, such as OutKast, Jay-Z, and Gucci Mane.

And I say that because we all could be a Dalai or Christ or Malcolm. We all have this greatness. It's a way to remind myself of that, as I listen to the record. And I don't even listen to it like it's me. The song is almost speaking *to* me. I mean, it's like me, but variations of me that have lived across time. When I'm an old man, hopefully, surrounded by my children and grandchildren, and great-grandchildren, that would be a record I'd want to hear as I meet my ancestors.

When I said, "Be like Coretta, or like Jackie Kennedy," I was actually speaking my deepest fears. As a man, you don't want your woman to be with another man because you've been assassinated or killed. At that time, I wasn't the Michael Render who helped Bernie Sanders. I wasn't a rapper who got a mayor elected in Atlanta. I knew this was who I was—a man who could die at any moment. It was a very audacious thing to say to the public. There have been times in the last year where I said, "You might get your head knocked off." It just puts me in touch with my own humanity—and the song is therapeutic to me to this day.

I'm in the gym every day and I tell myself I gotta get to eighty years old. My grandmother always said the Bible promises you three score and ten and everything after that is a bonus. When I picture myself dying, I'm surrounded by my family. I don't believe in the Abraham-ic concept of heaven and hell. I don't believe that I'm going to resurrect and go dance around with strangers. So if I want to transition to that next plane and go and be with my ancestors, I would like the lyrics of "Untitled" to be the last words I hear. That's the total culmination of who I am as a man. The physical piece of me that will one day lie dying in front of those I love is best embodied in that song.

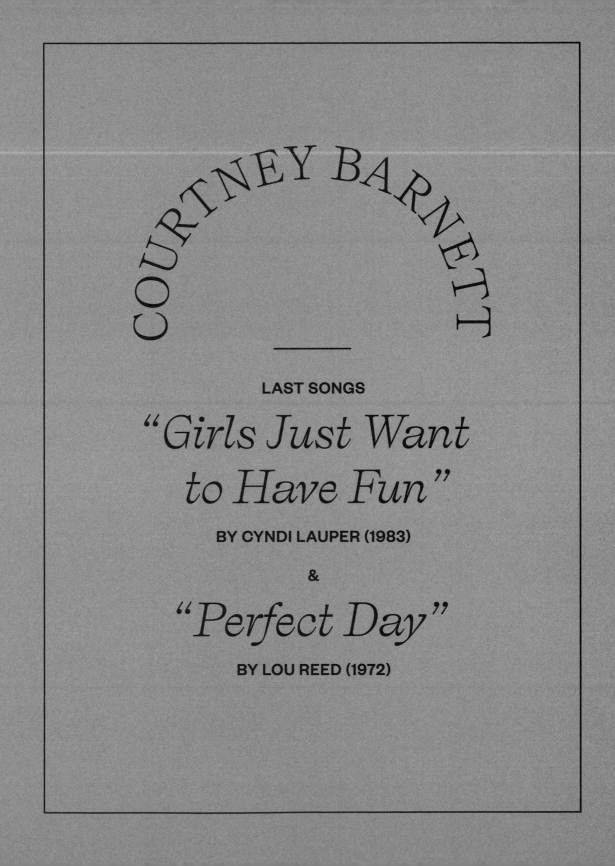

COURTNEY BARNETT

———

LAST SONGS

"Girls Just Want to Have Fun"

BY CYNDI LAUPER (1983)

&

"Perfect Day"

BY LOU REED (1972)

"Perfect Day"

ARTIST
Lou Reed

ALBUM
1972's *Transformer*

LENGTH
3 minutes, 45 seconds

FUN FACT
David Bowie played keyboards on, as well as coproduced, "Perfect Day."

IS "PERFECT DAY" ABOUT DEATH?
Who knows. Maybe. Depends on who you ask. And it depends on what you think of heroin. And whether or not this song is about heroin, which some people think it is. So if you interpret lines like "You just keep me hanging on" and "You're going to reap just what you sow" to be about heroin and you think heroin is a death sentence, then it's totally plausible that "Perfect Day" is about death.

Also, there's this: In a 2003 interview with the *Guardian*, Reed said, "You can't ask me to explain the lyrics because I won't do it."

T HIS IS A HARD ONE. IT'S A big decision. I think my natural inclination is a really sad, warm kinda song. Like Lou Reed's "Perfect Day." But then it's like, "Why didn't you pick something really happy?" Like "Girls Just Want to Have Fun"—Cyndi Lauper or something. It's like you need a mixtape. Not just one. The moments of the last hour of earth. I don't remember where I first heard Cyndi. I think it was probably when we had school dances, in primary school. I feel like there's a line of memory back to there. This nostalgic kind of feeling, a "toward the end of the night" song.

For me, Lou Reed was in my early twenties. I had just moved towns and had been in art school for a couple of years. I didn't really have much music and was just discovering new stuff. It was probably around that time. I moved to a new city with no job and was living on a couch in a friend's house. I was having a good time, but was a little bit lost.

I think my last song choices have a lot to do with that nostalgia bone in our body. A lot of the power of music is more about memory than the actual songs. A great structured song is all well and good, but the kind of memories that you build around it, the show that you sneak into with your friends when you're underage—that song from that band is always going to have so much more power over you than the greatest song written thirty years later. It's a funny thing when you think about it. I think the song holds the power of those memories.

I'm a hoarder and a collector. And songs capture a moment. I think there are people who are always wishing to go back to a period in time and that's unhealthy, not to live in the moment. I think it's important to look back and remember special moments, but to have a good balance.

"Girls Just Want to Have Fun"

ARTIST
Cyndi Lauper

ALBUM
She's So Unusual

LENGTH
3:58

CHART POSITION
No. 2 on the *Billboard* Hot 100, in March 1984

FUN FACT
The song was originally written and recorded in 1979 by Robert Hazard, a Philadelphia musician.

COURTNEY BARNETT

Courtney Barnett is an Australian rock musician. In 2016, she was nominated for the Best New Artist Grammy, and since releasing her debut album, *Sometimes I Sit and Think, and Sometimes I Just Sit*, in 2015, she's won five Australian Recording Industry Association Music Awards, including Best Rock Album for 2018's *Tell Me How You Really Feel*.

HOW TO PICK A SONG FOR YOUR FUNERAL

OUR FUNERAL IS AN EVENT ALWAYS LURKING somewhere in our mind, and maybe that's because of some deep-rooted narcissism—like, "Hey, there's essentially going to be a gathering, or party, or celebration *of my entire life*, and I can't even be there." So of course we'd want to have a bit of a say in it. And of course we'd want to dictate whether people can or cannot look at our creepy corpse, or whether an urn of ashes will be front and center. And of course we'd want to have first dibs on who is saying what. You want it to be people who will gush over you, tell a joke on your behalf, say what you meant to the world. To your family. To life.

And of course you'd want to have a killer playlist to accompany all this.

That's a lot of power and a lot of pressure, but a different kind of power and pressure than any other situation you'd be confronted with in your life. It's a last statement, in a way.

When famous musicians die, at times they will construct elaborate funerals with pretty incredible bouts of music woven throughout. Bouts that we could all learn something from and be inspired by.

YOU COULD:
HAVE SOMEONE SING FOR YOU

Want a surefire way to make your funeral memorable? Have phenomenal singers sing for your guests. At Johnny Cash's funeral in 2003, Sheryl Crow and Emmylou Harris sang the hymnal "The Old Rugged Cross" and Bob Dylan's "Every Grain of Sand."

At Biggie's funeral, Faith Evans sang "Walk with Me Lord."

And at Sam Cooke's funeral, Ray Charles sang "Angels Keep Watching Over Me."

OR YOU COULD:
HIRE YOUR FRIEND'S BAND

Perhaps having someone sing for you is a bit much—fine. You could always choose to rock out. When guitar god Jimi Hendrix unexpectedly passed away in September 1970, his funeral rightfully featured a live performance by the Buddy Miles Express. Miles had recently been playing with Hendrix—he was in his Band of Gypsys group—and, according to *Rolling Stone*, he played a full set at the funeral.

Janis Joplin went a bit further and paid for her own wake, hiring the Grateful Dead to play for roughly two hundred people.

WHAT ABOUT:
HAVING THAT ONE POIGNANT SONG PLAYED AND BRINGING EVERYONE TO TEARS

When Whitney Houston's casket was carried out of the church, her 1992 rendition of Dolly Parton's "I Will Always Love You" was played over the loudspeaker.

OMG. Can you imagine?

OR:
JUST HIRE STEVIE WONDER, THE MOST COVETED FUNERAL SINGER IN THE WORLD

If there was one singer you should zone in on hiring for your funeral, clearly it's Stevie Wonder. In the last thirty years, he's sung at the funerals of: Robin Williams, Whitney Houston, Nipsey Hussle, Aretha Franklin, Luther Vandross, James Cleveland, Ray Charles, Etta James, Gerald Levert, Andraé Crouch, Rick James, and Michael Jackson. Perhaps when one of your most celebrated albums is called *Songs in the Key of Life*, it's to be expected.

MAYBE, SCREW IT:
JUST PLAY "MY WAY"

For the last seventeen years, the Co-op Funeralcare, the UK's largest funeral provider service, has conducted research on the most popular songs played at funerals. Topping what they call "the funeral hot list" an impressive nine times? Frank Sinatra's "My Way."

"It's about having ups and downs and living life like you're supposed to," Nicola Meadows, a funeral director at the Co-op says about the song's funeral popularity. "The lyrics are suited to a funeral. It's a comfort not only to them, but family and friends."

Sure, sure, the music is pretty grandiose and has Ol' Blue Eyes singing about life and overcoming all the adversities—but don't expect it to be a triumphant moment. Meadows says people will break down. "It can be quite emotional and thought provoking. When you hear it, you think about an experience you shared with that person. You're not going to have any more of that, just memories," she says.

Okay, so your funeral songs are a pretty tall order.

C O-OP FUNERALCARE GATHERS DATA AND insights from their funeral directors and arrangers to come up with top-ten lists of songs people are playing at their funerals. They say these people oversee a hundred thousand funerals a year. That's a lot of death to manage. But also a lot of music.

Here's a more nuanced look at what songs are favored at funerals . . . at least in the UK, where the survey is conducted.

OVERALL

NO.	SONG	ARTIST
1	*"My Way"*	FRANK SINATRA
2	*"Time to Say Goodbye"*	ANDREA BOCELLI AND SARAH BRIGHTMAN
3	*"Over the Rainbow"*	EVA CASSIDY
4	*"Wind Beneath My Wings"*	BETTE MIDLER
5	*"Angels"*	ROBBIE WILLIAMS
6	*"Supermarket Flowers"*	ED SHEERAN
7	*"Unforgettable"*	NAT KING COLE
8	*"You Raise Me Up"*	WESTLIFE
9	*"We'll Meet Again"*	VERA LYNN
10	*"Always Look on the Bright Side of Life"*	ERIC IDLE from *Monty Python's Life of Brian*

INDIE

NO.	SONG	ARTIST
1	*"Chasing Cars"*	SNOW PATROL
2	*"Wonderwall"*	OASIS
3	*"Don't Look Back in Anger"*	OASIS
4	*"Live Forever"*	OASIS
5	*"One Day Like This"*	ELBOW
6	*"Bittersweet Symphony"*	VERVE
7	*"Fix You"*	COLDPLAY
8	*"Mr. Brightside"*	THE KILLERS
9	*"Paradise"*	COLDPLAY
10	*"Clocks"*	COLDPLAY

CONTEMPORARY/POP

NO.	SONG	ARTIST
1	*"Angels"*	ROBBIE WILLIAMS
2	*"You Raise Me Up"*	WESTLIFE
3	*"Supermarket Flowers"*	ED SHEERAN
4	*"See You Again"*	WIZ KHALIFA
5	*"Dancing Queen"*	ABBA
6	*"Lay Me Down"*	SAM SMITH
7	*"Dancing in the Sky"*	DANI AND LIZZY
8	*"Flying Without Wings"*	WESTLIFE
9	*"How Long Will I Love You"*	ELLIE GOULDING
10	*"7 Years"*	LUKAS GRAHAM

ROCK

NO.	SONG	ARTIST
1	*"Stairway to Heaven"*	LED ZEPPELIN
2	*"Bat Out of Hell"*	MEATLOAF
3	*"Don't Wanna Miss a Thing"*	AEROSMITH
4	*"Who Wants to Live Forever"*	QUEEN
5	*"The Show Must Go On"*	QUEEN
6	*"Knocking on Heaven's Door"*	GUNS N' ROSES
7	*"Wish You Were Here"*	PINK FLOYD
8	*"Highway to Hell"*	AC/DC
9	*"Another One Bites the Dust"*	QUEEN
10	*"Bohemian Rhapsody"*	QUEEN

COUNTRY

NO.	SONG	ARTIST
1	*"I Will Always Love You"*	DOLLY PARTON
2	*"Islands in the Stream"*	DOLLY PARTON AND KENNY ROGERS
3	*"Country Roads"*	JOHN DENVER
4	*"9 to 5"*	DOLLY PARTON
5	*"If Tomorrow Never Comes"*	GARTH BROOKS
6	*"Annie's Song"*	JOHN DENVER
7	*"Ring of Fire"*	JOHNNY CASH
8	*"When I Get Where I'm Going"*	DOLLY PARTON AND BRAD PAISLEY
9	*"Stand by Your Man"*	DOLLY PARTON
10	*"The Gambler"*	KENNY ROGERS

R&B

NO.	SONG	ARTIST
1	*"I'll Be Missing You"*	PUFF DADDY (Featuring Faith Evans & 112)
2	*"I Miss You"*	BEYONCÉ
3	*"One Sweet Day"*	MARIAH CAREY & BOYZ II MEN
4	*"Dance with My Father Again"*	LUTHER VANDROSS
5	*"It's So Hard to Say Goodbye to Yesterday"*	BOYZ II MEN
6	*"Killing Me Softly"*	THE FUGEES
7	*"Because I Got High"*	AFROMAN
8	*"Blinded by Your Grace"*	STORMZY
9	*"Call Out My Name"*	THE WEEKND
10	*"I'll Be Missing You"*	CHAKA DEMUS & PLIERS

JAZZ

NO.	SONG	ARTIST
1	*"What a Wonderful World"*	LOUIS ARMSTRONG
2	*"Ain't No Sunshine"*	BILL WITHERS
3	*"In the Mood"*	GLENN MILLER
4	*"Smile"*	NAT KING COLE
5	*"When the Saints Go Marching In"*	VARIOUS
6	*"At Last"*	ETTA JAMES
7	*"Take 5"*	DAVE BRUBECK
8	*"Unforgettable"*	NAT KING COLE
9	*"The Thrill Is Gone"*	B. B. KING
10	*"Begin the Beguine"*	ARTIE SHAW

HYMNS

NO.	SONG
1	*"Abide with Me"*
2	*"All Things Bright and Beautiful"*
3	*"The Lord Is My Shepherd"*
4	*"How Great Thou Art"*
5	*"Amazing Grace"*
6	*"Jerusalem"*
7	*"Morning Has Broken"*
8	*"Old Rugged Cross"*
9	*"The Day Thou Gavest"*
10	*"Calon Lan"*

CLASSICAL

NO.	SONG	ARTIST
1	*"Nimrod"*	EDWARD ELGAR
2	*"Time to Say Goodbye"*	ANDREA BOCELLI AND SARAH BRIGHTMAN
3	*"Canon in D"*	JOHANN PACHELBEL
4	*"Ave Maria"*	FRANZ SCHUBERT
5	*"The Lark Ascending"*	RALPH VAUGHAN WILLIAMS
6	*"Pie Jesu"*	GABRIEL FAURÉ
7	*"Adagio for Strings"*	SAMUEL BARBER
8	*"Air on the G String"*	JOHANN SEBASTIAN BACH
9	*"Four Seasons"*	ANTONIO VIVALDI
10	*"Clair de Lune"*	CLAUDE DEBUSSY

BOBB BRUNO

BEST COAST

LAST SONG

"Laughter in the Rain"

BY NEIL SEDAKA (1974)

GROWING UP HISPANIC IN LOS ANGELES, I was baptized Catholic and went to a couple religious schools. But then from third grade to about sixth grade, I was in a Lutheran school. We had chapel every Wednesday, and that was a Bible-heavy environment. At that age, I was into the Bible and learning about God and the usual stuff that goes along with that. But once I got out of there, I went to a Montessori school and that's when I started to think that all the Bible stuff wasn't something that was going to happen. These weren't things that happened in the history of man. That's when I became an atheist. It would be cool if there was something afterward that was pleasant. But I don't necessarily expect that to happen.

"Laughter in the Rain"

ARTIST
Neil Sedaka

ALBUM
Sedaka's Back, a collection of singles Elton John's label put together to reintroduce Neil to the United States

LENGTH
2 minutes, 46 seconds

CHART POSITION
No. 1 on the Billboard Hot 100 on February 1, 1975

IS THIS SONG ABOUT DEATH?
Not at all. "Laughter in the Rain" was a collaboration between Sedaka and, at the time, the unknown songwriter Phil Cody. Sedaka did the music, Cody mainly did the lyrics. And "Laughter in the Rain" was written in upstate New York, after Cody got high and dozed off under a tree. He was feeling a bit of writer's block and was pining for a girl back in New York City he'd just gotten together with. And the lyrics reflect that: it's a meditation on how something like rain, which people can associate with being a buzzkill, can be a joyous experience.

BOBB BRUNO

Multi-instrumentalist Bobb Bruno formed indie-rock band Best Coast with Bethany Cosentino in 2009. The band has played extensively throughout the United States and Europe and has shared bills with Weezer, Paramore, and Green Day. Their latest album is *Always Tomorrow*, released in 2020.

My last song was originally going to be something heavy, like Wilco's "On and On and On." Because that song *is* about dying. But I've decided I want it to be "Laughter in the Rain" by Neil Sedaka. There are a lot of reasons. But the number one reason is that I just really do love that song. I listen to it all the time. The second reason is that, as much as I appreciate the song, I realize that it's probably the most blatant rip-off of "Waterloo Sunset" by the Kinks, which is also really amusing to me. Also, it reminds me of a friend—she had never heard it and I played it for her. And now she's obsessed with it. Probably on a weekly basis, she'll post short Instagram clips of her singing it really loudly in a car. Those always make me laugh. "Laughter in the Rain" is just a good vibe no matter what my mood is. The lyrics are so relaxing—Sedaka's singing about a real nice scenario!

It's hard for me to remember when I first heard it. But it had to have been when I was a little kid, growing up in the seventies. It was always on the radio. After that, it was featured in a TV ad for a local soft-rock station and those Time Life *AM Gold* infomercials. I was obsessed with infomercials for a period of time; there were so many and I'd watch them as if they were television shows. There was a sixties-themed one I was into, and also "Freedom Rock." I was super into "Freedom Rock." But that *AM Gold* one was a big favorite of mine and I know that's a big part of this origin story.

Listen to it. The harmony vocals and chorus are really beautiful. The piano intro, too, is really cool. That is unique. But once the verse kicks in, it's a total "Waterloo Sunset" rip-off.

48

49

ANDRÉ 3000

"Sometimes It Snows in April"

BY PRINCE (1986)

I'M A PESSIMIST; I ALWAYS THINK OF THE worst. I'm always thinking of death in some way. In recent years, my parents and my stepdad passed away, so it's been a little bit of funeral fatigue. This is reality now. The older we get, the more funerals we're going to. I'm forty-five right now as I'm giving this answer, and I have had to start thinking of things I never had to think about before. I never planned on being an adult. Sometimes, I'm looking around and I'm like, "Damn, I have to be an adult. Fuck!"

"Sometimes It Snows in April"

ARTIST
Prince

ALBUM
Parade, which was also the soundtrack to his 1986 directorial debut, *Under the Cherry Moon.*

LENGTH
6 minutes, 49 seconds

RECORDING DATE
April 21, 1985—thirty-one years prior to the day Prince died in 2016

IS THIS SONG ABOUT DEATH?
Very much so. The song details the death of Prince's character, Christopher Tracy, and what he's likely doing in heaven now.

ANDRÉ 3000

André 3000 was a co-founder of hip-hop duo OutKast, a pioneer of southern rap. He does everything these days, from acting, to music, to fashion design.

When I was younger, I heard "Sometimes It Snows in April" by Prince. That was always a song that summed up what it is. Usually, when someone dies, unless they die of old age or sickness—it happens in a strange way. Both of my parents are gone and they both died early. Just out of the blue, when I least expected it. Even the lyrics "Sometimes it snows in April" is kind of like . . . it's not the time it's supposed to snow. So it means something really serious happened when it wasn't expected. The mood of the song always clicked in that sort of way. I never knew what Prince was talking about, but it sounded like he was talking about a life.

I got into Prince in my early teens. My older cousin, I looked up to him and he had all the girls, all the cool clothes. His girlfriends would come over and they'd hang out. And I got into Prince because he was into Prince. And I'm listening to it—and I'm like, *What the hell?* You know Prince: he expands and goes into any kinda music. And my cousin, he was the coolest dude I knew at the time, so this Prince dude, he gotta be cool. I didn't really *connect connect* to it until I got a little older, like in my late teens, when I started to understand the lyrics a little bit more. To be more concerned with the lyrics. Ever since then, Prince is like an oasis for me. He showed a whole generation you can make any type of music you want. And that's what it's about. Prince represented that to me more than anything. It's all music. Just do it.

When I was younger, me and my friend were in a car accident. We were riding with my friend's mom, but we were so young, we didn't know what happened until we woke up in the hospital. I didn't know. I was a kid. Fortunately, we were on this street in Atlanta and it was a non-busy street. And fortunately this guy who had money passed by—and he had one of the first working cell phones. It was like a suitcase. And he was able to call an ambulance. If we didn't have that cell phone, we would have been out there for a minute—and might have died. Who knows. I don't know if that's a near-death experience. But I was definitely lucky.

WAYNE COYNE

THE FLAMING LIPS

LAST SONG

"What a Wonderful World"

BY LOUIS ARMSTRONG (1967)

A T DIFFERENT TIMES IN MY LIFE I'VE thought about this thing and how fucking horribly tragic that would be—that you would get to pick your last song. Jesus Christ. That's about as devastating as you can get! Let's say I'm getting electrocuted or whatever I'm dying of: I'm going to be dead, but do the people around me know it's the last song? Or am I listening to it on headphones, in isolation, as I get taken to the electric chair?

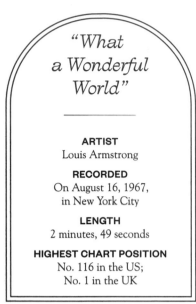

"What a Wonderful World"

ARTIST
Louis Armstrong

RECORDED
On August 16, 1967,
in New York City

LENGTH
2 minutes, 49 seconds

HIGHEST CHART POSITION
No. 116 in the US;
No. 1 in the UK

It's tough. Music does that great thing but also that horrible thing where it takes emotions and your life and just crescendos it up for two or three minutes and it's fucking devastating. Depending on your song and your mood, when you get done with your song, you kinda wanna kill yourself. And then you want to live more than ever, all at the same time. It's an absurd, overwhelming connection for your whole life. Everything that's ever happened to you is in this stream. So part of you thinks, do you really want that song, whatever it is for you? And then you just go get electrocuted? Or is it that you want that song and it's an overwhelming feeling of all this love from your family or children or whatever. That will be a tough choice. Are you listening to it for yourself? Or to remember someone or something else?

When we do a Flaming Lips show, almost every night when we get done and can control what we play on the PA, we play Louis Armstrong's "What a Wonderful World." It's special to me, but I know everybody plays it. This is a song that goes in and out of being so sentimental, powerless—and some other times, it's so powerful, it devastates you. And so in a sense, I would hope I don't get to pick my last song. But I think people would pick something like that. It's probably these types of emotionally connective songs.

To me, it's Louis who's doing it. When you think of the plight of his life—I think he's sincere, that smile he would do. His singing is so weird. We've all gotten used to it, but it's so fucking weird. I don't know. There's a couple of songs that all the songwriters wish they'd written and this is one of them. It's perfect, but it's also perfect because he's doing it.

Almost every show we play, someone will tell us about using the song "Do You Realize??" at their grandmother's funeral or the birth of their kids. For songwriters, that's as great as it can possibly ever get. To know you're with their

WAYNE COYNE

Wayne Coyne has been the front-man for the Flaming Lips since 1983. Over the years, the band has constantly found innovative ways to get music to their fans, including encased in limited-edition candy gummy skulls and actual (real) human skulls. They've performed at festivals, clubs, and theaters all over the world.

people. When we play these songs live, we never do them like, "Ugh, that song again." Someone in the audience—they've been waiting for that song. It's not just another moment. We have a few of those. For me personally, if I heard the song "Do You Realize??" I'm not sure it would affect me. I know it affects other people. And I know it's something about the mystery of those chord changes and my way of singing, which is very fragile sometimes. I'm not even always aware of it.

So my last song would be something like "What a Wonderful World" or "Over the Rainbow." One of those deep, hokey songs. I don't have any song that has meaning for me that wouldn't have meaning for anybody else. Most of the songs I'm enjoying, I'm enjoying because everybody around me is enjoying them, too.

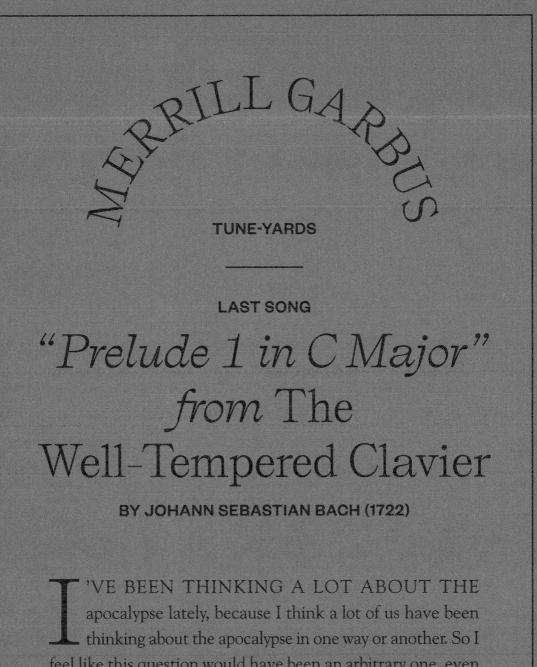

MERRILL GARBUS

TUNE-YARDS

———

LAST SONG

"Prelude 1 in C Major" *from* The Well-Tempered Clavier

BY JOHANN SEBASTIAN BACH (1722)

I'VE BEEN THINKING A LOT ABOUT THE apocalypse lately, because I think a lot of us have been thinking about the apocalypse in one way or another. So I feel like this question would have been an arbitrary one, even ten years ago. But now it feels a little more real. I don't mean to be melodramatic about the world ending—I don't think it's going to happen like that. But it just became more real.

"*Prelude*
1 in C Major"
from
The
Well-Tempered
Clavier

ARTIST
Bach

ALBUM IT APPEARED ON
None. He wrote it on sheet music
back around 1722.

**WTF DOES
"WELL-TEMPERED" MEAN?
WAS BACH A HOTHEAD?**
In this case, *well-tempered* was what
music theorists said Bach meant
when he was describing how a piece
could work in all keys. Fascinating!

The first thing that came to me was Bach's *Well-Tempered Clavier*. It's music I grew up on. The very first Key of C—I think it's Prelude 1 in Key of C—and that was partially because that's the music I was literally born into. My mom is a piano player and she, as a pianist, was practicing those pieces when I was in the womb. I feel like that is what gives me the immediate reaction of "Of course that would be the very last music I'd ever want to hear."

Even talking about it, I could cry. Even considering the first notes . . . it nearly always brings me to tears when I hear them. I think it's something about how simple it begins; it really does feel like a beginning. It feels circular. It's a repetition of eight notes. But then the notes shift and change throughout the piece and it becomes really complex, really harmonically complex, just in that one piece. And then it goes through drama; there's so much emotional drama just in those notes. Then it cycles back to the very first chords. In and of itself, it's this circular song.

I feel really confused these days. I forget sometimes that up until this point, a lot of me has been thinking that someday things are going to make sense. And in fact, nothing makes sense and it's more confusing than ever before. And yet, if I can really root down to why I'm alive—this question that you're asking us—it is to consider death. And that's something crucial that we think about a lot in a panicky way, but also don't consider enough.

In my household when I was growing up, music was the closest thing to religion that we practiced. And my parents speak about music, and practice music, in the ways that I see other people speak about religion and God and spirituality. So having something that reminds me of my connection to my parents and ancestors deeper than that, when I die, also feels really spiritual. When I'm in doubt, I can go back to that song. Being close to death, and experiencing the

MERRILL GARBUS

Oakland, California based Merrill Garbus records under the name Tune-Yards with her partner, Nate Brenner. Since forming in 2006, Tune-Yards has released four albums and recently started composing for film: the 2018 breakout film *Sorry to Bother You* features a Tune-Yards score.

fear and doubt, but knowing that I can once again come back to that piece of music, is very comforting.

I think about how attached I am to people liking me. I'm trying to detach from that. But when we're performing and putting art into the world, there's a reaching out that an artist does for a connection. And often, I think that's in a form of "Do you like me?" "Won't you like me?" It's interesting to think about that. There are songs and pieces that I don't feel a connection to. But it's not about that. It's not about everyone selecting the same song. It's almost like that's the magic of music—it doesn't make sense. It's a big mystery on how all those dots get connected. How it was that my mother became a pianist and then it became part of her life to practice this one piece, in the time of her life, when she was pregnant. And this German composer in the 1700s who wrote this piece—all the things that have to come together, for my human attachment to that series of sounds.

I can play this. It's one of the things I wanted to learn when I started taking piano, and it's one of the things that I can play by memory. It's really a hard piece for me to play by ear. I don't read music easily and I mostly try to play it by ear. It's not intuitive and in a way is more complex than a prelude in C might be. It feels like a metaphor for trying really hard. I have to struggle a little bit. It doesn't have that constant, cyclical nature yet. But whenever I start playing it, I start to feel a zen centering.

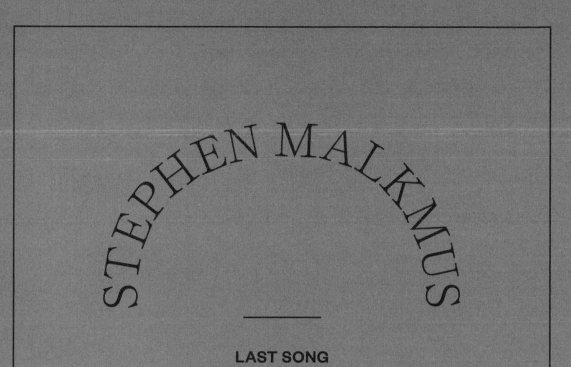

STEPHEN MALKMUS

———

LAST SONG

"*Carefree Highway*"

BY GORDON LIGHTFOOT (1974)

O BVIOUSLY, YOU'D WANT TO PLAY something you share with the ones you love. It's almost not about you—you imagine yourself on your deathbed, and that spirit is plucking out from you. Everyone's around your bed, because I don't think anyone wants to die alone. You get that feeling, as your parents are getting older, they want you there—and that's maybe one reason they even had you.

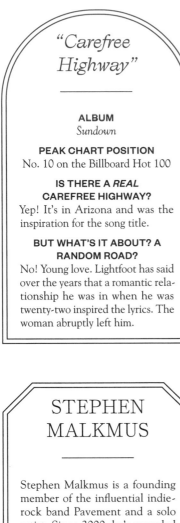

"Carefree Highway"

ALBUM
Sundown

PEAK CHART POSITION
No. 10 on the Billboard Hot 100

**IS THERE A *REAL*
CAREFREE HIGHWAY?**
Yep! It's in Arizona and was the
inspiration for the song title.

**BUT WHAT'S IT ABOUT? A
RANDOM ROAD?**
No! Young love. Lightfoot has said
over the years that a romantic relationship he was in when he was
twenty-two inspired the lyrics. The
woman abruptly left him.

STEPHEN MALKMUS

Stephen Malkmus is a founding
member of the influential indie-
rock band Pavement and a solo
artist. Since 2000, he's recorded
and released seven albums with his
band the Jicks, as well as two solo
records.

So my song would be something related to my family, a song that we all share, in a way. I wouldn't want it to be sad, but I'm not going to put "Lucky" by Daft Punk, which is a song we all like. That's too frivolous. Or "Blank Space," because my daughter doesn't even like Taylor Swift anymore.

There's a song by Gordon Lightfoot called "Carefree Highway." My kids always get very sad when we play this song, because, well, it's a sad song. But I played a benefit for a friend of mine who died prematurely of cancer. She was alive then—and it wasn't a certain outcome at the time, and we did a benefit for her. My daughter and I sang that song. I don't know why, except that I'd like to be Gordon Lightfoot and write some of his songs. So I'll say that. Even though it's kinda sad. Even though I would want something not as melancholy-sounding, I've led to that.

Gordon Lightfoot occupies in my mind above the other singer-songwriters of the seventies. He's masculine, but it doesn't feel macho. It's sensitive, but not completely self-pitying. There's an outsider vibe to it, in my opinion. It didn't have to be, but people just liked it.

STEPHEN MALKMUS

FAMOUS MUSICIANS AND THE LAST LIVE SONGS THEY PLAYED

LOOKING AT THE LAST SONGS MUSICIANS played live, you'll notice that for a majority of our beloved cultural icons, they were performing pretty much up until the day they died. Okay, not literally the next day—but one moment they were there, doing what they spent their whole life doing in front of an audience, only to exit the big stage left weeks or months later. And sometimes it was just days.

No one ever goes to a concert thinking, "Wow, this could be the last time I'm ever going to get to see this artist." And no one ever goes to a concert thinking, "Wow, this could be the last time *anyone* gets to see this artist." But both of those scenarios could literally happen to anyone at any moment, which is a weird thing to think about. And thinking about concerts and shows like that—well, perhaps it would make us savor the experience all a bit more.

Let's take a look at the different types of last live songs of some famous musicians.

ARTISTS WHO WENT OUT PLAYING THEIR HIT

For many famous musicians, the last song they ever played was a big-time hit. And it makes sense. Why? Because of course you're going to encore with something everyone knows. You want them to come back the next time, right?

ELVIS PRESLEY

LAST SHOW
June 26, 1977

VENUE
Market Square Arena,
Indianapolis, Indiana

DIED
August 16, 1977

LAST SONG
"Can't Help Falling
in Love"

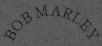

BOB MARLEY

LAST SHOW
September 23, 1980

VENUE
Stanley Theatre,
Pittsburgh, Pennsylvania

DIED
May 11, 1981

LAST SONG
"Get Up, Stand Up"

PRINCE

LAST SHOW
April 14, 2016

VENUE
Fox Theatre,
Atlanta, Georgia

DIED
April 21, 2016

LAST SONG
"Purple Rain"/"Beautiful
Ones"/"Diamonds
& Pearls" medley

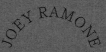

JOEY RAMONE

LAST SHOW
December 11, 2000

VENUE
Continental,
New York City

DIED
April 15, 2001

LAST SONG
"Blitzkrieg Bop"

JIMI HENDRIX

LAST SHOW
September 6, 1970

VENUE
Open Air Love
& Peace Festival,
Fehmarn, Germany

DIED
September 18, 1970

LAST SONG
"Voodoo Child"

FREDDIE MERCURY

LAST SHOW
August 9, 1986

VENUE
Knebworth House,
Knebworth, England

DIED
November 24, 1991

LAST SONG
"We Are the Champions"

JOHN BONHAM

LAST SHOW
July 7, 1980

VENUE
Eissporthalle,
Berlin, Germany

DIED
September 25, 1980

LAST SONG
"Whole Lotta Love"

TOM PETTY

LAST SHOW
September 25, 2017

VENUE
Hollywood Bowl, Los
Angeles, California

DIED
October 2, 2017

LAST SONG
"American Girl"

ARETHA FRANKLIN

LAST SHOW
November 7, 2017

VENUE
Cathedral of St. John
the Divine—Elton
John's AIDS Foundation
25th Annual Gala

DIED
August 16, 2018

LAST SONG
"Freeway of Love"

MARVIN GAYE

LAST SHOW
August 14, 1983

VENUE
Pacific Amphitheatre,
Costa Mesa, California

DIED
April 1, 1984

LAST SONG
"Sexual Healing"

ADAM YAUCH

LAST SHOW
June 12, 2009

VENUE
Bonnaroo Music
and Arts Festival,
Manchester, Tennessee

DIED
May 4, 2012

LAST SONG
"Sabotage"

TUPAC

LAST SHOW
July 4, 1996

VENUE
House of Blues
Sunset Strip, West
Hollywood, California

DIED
September 13, 1996

LAST SONG
"2 of Amerikaz
Most Wanted"

KURT COBAIN

LAST SHOW
March 1, 1994

VENUE
Terminal 1, Munich,
Germany

DIED
April 5, 1994

LAST SONG
"Heart-Shaped Box"

ARTISTS WHO PLAYED A COVER SONG

Paying tribute to someone else is of course a time-honored tradition that most bands and artists have done at one point or another in their musical careers. These artists' last songs weren't their own—but they were masters of making everything they played sound like their own.

ELLIOTT SMITH

LAST SHOW
September 9, 2003

VENUE
University of Utah,
Salt Lake City, Utah

DIED
October 21, 2003

LAST SONG
"Long, Long, Long"
(the Beatles)

JOHN COLTRANE

LAST SHOW
May 7, 1967

VENUE
Famous Ballroom,
Baltimore, Maryland

DIED
July 17, 1967

LAST SONG
"I Want to Talk
About You" (Billy
Eckstine cover)

CLARENCE CLEMONS

LAST SHOW
December 7, 2010

VENUE
Carousel House, Asbury
Park, New Jersey

DIED
June 18, 2011

LAST SONG
"Blue Christmas"
(written by Billy Hayes
and Jay W. Johnson;
made famous by Elvis)

LEONARD COHEN

LAST SHOW
December 21, 2013

VENUE
Vector Arena, Auckland,
New Zealand

DIED
November 7, 2016

LAST SONG
"Save the Last Dance
for Me" (written by
Doc Pomus and Mort
Shuman; made famous
by the Drifters)

WHEN THE LAST SONG WAS A BIT PROPHETIC

Of course, when you're up onstage, you'd never think, *This is the last thing I'll ever be playing in front of people.* But perhaps someone or something somewhere else knows differently?

JIM MORRISON

LAST SHOW
December 12, 1970

VENUE
The Warehouse, New
Orleans, Louisiana

DIED
July 3, 1971

LAST SONG
"The End"

LEVON HELM

LAST SHOW
March 24, 2012

VENUE
Tarrytown Music Hall,
Tarrytown, New York

DIED
April 19, 2012

LAST SONG
"Gloryland"

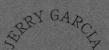

JERRY GARCIA

LAST SHOW
July 9, 1995

VENUE
Soldier Field,
Chicago, Illinois

DIED
August 9, 1995

LAST SONG
"Box of Rain"

CHRIS CORNELL

LAST SHOW
May 17, 2017

VENUE
Fox Theatre,
Detroit, Michigan

DIED
May 18, 2017

LAST SONG
"Slaves and Bulldozers"
(with Led Zeppelin's
"In My Time of Dying"
verses weaved in)

CURTIS MAYFIELD

LAST SHOW
July 7, 1990

VENUE
Central Park
SummerStage, NYC

DIED
December 26, 1999

LAST SONG
"When Seasons Change"

WHEN THE LAST SONG WAS WITH SOMEBODY ELSE

Some artists' last performances weren't at one of their own shows at all. So if you were witnessing this—it was by pure luck.

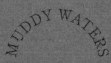

DAVID BOWIE

LAST SHOW
November 9, 2006

VENUE
Hammerstein Ballroom, New York City, Benefit for the Keep a Child Alive organization

DIED
January 10, 2016

LAST SONG
"Changes" (with Alicia Keys)

LOU REED

LAST SHOW
March 6, 2013 (performing during an Antony and the Johnsons show)

VENUE
Salle Pleyel, Paris, France

DIED
October 27, 2013

LAST SONG
"Candy Says"

MUDDY WATERS

LAST SHOW
June 30, 1982 (performing with Eric Clapton & His Band)

VENUE
Hollywood Sportatorium, Pembroke Pines, Florida

DIED
April 30, 1983

LAST SONG
"Blow Wind Blow"

WHEN THE LAST PERFORMANCE WAS ON TV

For some artists, their last proper live performance was a scaled-back affair—instead of a concert, they last graced a TV soundstage. In each of these cases, finality wasn't top of mind during the performance, but in the end, it was captured for a bigger audience to see (and now anyone, thanks to YouTube).

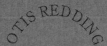

OTIS REDDING

LAST SHOW
December 9, 1967

VENUE
Upbeat, WEWS-TV Cleveland

DIED
December 10, 1967

LAST SONG
"Knock on Wood" (written by Eddie Floyd & Steve Cropper)

JOHN LENNON

LAST SHOW
April 18, 1975

VENUE
Hilton Hotel Grand Ballroom, New York City—the Salute to Sir Lew taping

DIED
December 8, 1980

LAST SONG
"Imagine"

GEORGE HARRISON

LAST SHOW
July 24, 1997

VENUE
VH1 Studios

DIED
November 29, 2001

LAST SONG
"All Things Must Pass"

AALIYAH

LAST SHOW
July 25, 2001

VENUE
The Tonight Show with Jay Leno

DIED
August 25, 2001

LAST SONG
"More Than a Woman"

69

MATT BERNINGER

THE NATIONAL

———

LAST SONG

"Hang Down Your Head"

&

"Time"

BY TOM WAITS (1985)

I WENT THROUGH A *RAIN DOGS* PHASE AND a Tom Waits phase, in and out, all the time. *Rain Dogs* for a million reasons—there was a woman I was with in college who had it. Tom is being so mothered, so sweetly, on the cover, and that crazy name: *Rain Dogs*. That's when I did a deep dive. Of all the Tom Waits records, it's probably the one I chewed on the most. "Hang Down Your Head" is like a poppy breakup song.

He wrote it with his wife, Kathleen Brennan, and it's so cool. Just abstract, thrown together. Like they're seeing mumbled things. "Hush a wild violet, hush a band of gold / Hush you're in a story I heard somebody told." It's just so beautiful and quiet and it's this little pop song. This little morsel. It feels very effortless.

And then "Time" follows it up. It's just filled with a series of beautiful images. You jump from surreal postcard to surreal postcard, and somehow it makes this incredible sense at the end. I've always thought it must be a song about death. But it's not. "It's time, time, time that you love" is the chorus. I always thought it was "It's time, time, time that you live." I always remember mishearing it as "live." But it's "love." Time that you love. Time that you start letting love in, and loving yourself. It's just one of these things that I can't totally understand. It starts out with "Well, the smart money's on Harlow." I don't know who Harlow is. And I don't care. I don't care about the place necessarily, either—"east of east St. Louis" or wherever. These dominos of thought tumble into each other. But then it slows down: "It's time, time, time to love."

When I hear these, I think to myself that I've stolen every single line and rearranged it somewhere, and put it somewhere in a National song. Every single line I think, "Oh, I ripped that off from this other line." They are songs that I've excavated subconsciously: totally stripped bare of their parts and reused.

"Time" is trying to connect with everything. It's trying to understand these tiny moments that belong to all these people. Napoleon's in the song! There are kids jumping off of cars and splashing in the streets. What is that? There's a woman who kills a thousand pigeons with a razor from her boot. Your mind just gets blown with these beautiful things. Sad stuff and super-beautiful stuff. "So put a candle in a window and a kiss upon his lips." It sounds like it could be from the cheesiest song ever written, yet there's the lady that killed all the pigeons. He takes these turns in that song and it just feels like that's the way life is. One minute you can see something awful, and one minute someone could kiss you on the lips. That's why the song works. And it keeps reminding you that it's time to be loved. What else can you say? It's one of those haunting ones.

"Hang Down Your Head" and "Time" . . . Hearing them, loving them, I probably never thought about it until now. What is it about those songs? Then you sit there and read the lyrics and read the context and you realize he put them in a sequence, where he was wearing big outfits. Caricatures. *Rain Dogs* comes out with all these vaudevillian, fetish characters. And then all of a sudden "Hang Down Your Head" and "Time"—it's just Tom Waits. He's not putting on any show here. It's all coming right from him, who you think Tom Waits probably is.

I write songs with my wife a lot. We've written more and more collaboratively over the years. The first time we thought we wrote a song together happened on *Boxer*. When I was thinking about this question, I popped onto Wikipedia to do a little digging, and I think "Hang Down Your Head" was the first song Tom Waits co-credits with Kathleen Brennan. I love thinking about which were her lines and which were his. Of course, this song connects with me! It's about a woman named Marie. His wife's name is Kathleen. So they came up with a name to protect her probably—but of course it's Kathleen! It can't be anyone else. My wife, Carin, and I have done that so many times. Karen. Ada. Vanderlyle is probably my wife. Rylan is my wife, I think. And my daughter. "Hang Down Your Head" is the first song they wrote together—they take a person's name—and just throw some lines at each other and put a melody to it.

MATT BERNINGER

Matt Berninger is the frontman and vocalist of the National, one of the biggest indie-rock bands of the past twenty years. He also starred in *Mistaken for Strangers*, a "rock-doc" directed by his brother Tom, which premiered at the Tribeca Film Festival. The National's 2017 album *Sleep Well Beast* won the Grammy for Best Alternative Album.

I don't know what art is if it's not your real stuff. So what are you doing? Writing about other people? Or just trying for songs like they're public service announcements? I don't know what people are writing about if they're not writing about their deepest loves, their deepest fears—their own. The real ones. You put them into these characters, you put them into these moments, and you make something beautiful out of it. "Hang Down Your Head" is a very sad song. One of our songs is "Sorrow." I know I stole from Bowie for that one. I steal from everything, including my wife. And vice versa. She does the same. So yeah, it's also like, "What is love about?" Love is about when you connect with somebody and you empathize and you see yourself in them and they see themselves in you. And you say, "I like you, you like me, I feel safe with you." You make me feel braver and happier. Let's create something together. A family. A record. A movie. Whatever. It's that connection between people . . . that's love. So art and love in my mind are kind of synonymous.

The connections between art and people . . . it's like, you like that and I like that, "Let's make a band." It's how you meet your friends. It's how you talk to people. Even if you have no friends, you hear people like Michael Stipe and Morrissey and Kim Deal, people you never met, who can make something awesome out of all the same anxieties you have. And you love them. And you feel loved by that record. And that someone reached out to you. And they did! They got together, they made some stuff. It's hard to write your first song, it's hard to write your tenth song, it's hard to write a record, and these people did. There's usually zero reward for it. If you're really lucky, other people will like it, too. Often people start bands because they can't even talk to their own parents. They have to talk to the rest of the world and hope someone answers.

Music studios, art studios, music classes and art classes in high school, and rock venues are the churches where we tell the truth and reach out to God. And we find God in our friends, in the people we find that with. Some people find God in a religious institution or in a sports team. But for me, it's in records. And radio stations. And rock clubs. And in bars.

So these two songs—"Hang Down Your Head" and "Time"—are embedded in my soul. I probably don't even need to hear them again. And I think the afterlife is what you leave behind—or what you do every day. You cut somebody off in traffic and gave somebody the finger—it's like, what'd you do? Did you make the universe more like heaven or more like hell? We're all living in our own heavens and hells, all in the now. When my body is gone, when my consciousness is off—that's just the bag, the container. The real me is already all over the place. You're continuously painting your own afterlife. When I'm gone, somebody is going to be a little bit Matt Berninger.

ARTIST
Tom Waits

ALBUM THEY APPEAR ON
Rain Dogs

RECORDED
1985, New York City

LENGTH
2 minutes, 32 seconds; and
3 minutes, 55 seconds

DOES TOM WAITS KNOW WHAT "HANG DOWN YOUR HEAD" IS ABOUT?
Unclear: On Waits's 1999 VH1 Storytellers appearance, he tells the crowd he wrote the song when he was seven. He also said, "Some of these I don't remember where they came from. But I'll make something up, it might be better. It's kinda like when you're at the movies and you're watching a really bad film and someone leans in and says, 'You know, this is a true story.' Does it really improve the film?"

DOES TOM WAITS KNOW WHAT "TIME" IS ABOUT?
Unclear: When he promoted Rain Dogs on Letterman in 1986, he sang the song after doing an interview where he didn't talk about "Time" or any songs and instead extensively discussed being born in the back of a cab, his feelings about New York, and filming Jim Jarmusch's Down by Law.

75

MARGO PRICE

LAST SONG

"A Day in the Life"

BY THE BEATLES (1967)

I N COLLEGE, SOMEBODY HAD GIVEN ME AN ounce of mushrooms—it was actually an ex-boyfriend of mine. He drove them up to me so I could sell them to all my friends during Halloween week. He said, "I gotta tell you, these things are really strong." They were white with blue stripes going through them. He was like, "Some people who have taken acid and psychedelics many times have had freak-outs on these. So don't take too many."

"A Day in the Life"

ARTIST
The Beatles

ALBUM
Sgt. Pepper's Lonely
Hearts Club Band

RECORDED
January and February 1967

LENGTH
5:37

IS THIS SONG ABOUT DEATH?
John Lennon is said to have been literally singing about someone dying. Who is that someone? Tara Browne, the heir to the Guinness brewery fortune. He died at the age of twenty-one in a car crash, about a month before the first recording session of "A Day in the Life" took place—Lennon said he was reading the news story in the *Daily Mail* when he wrote the lines about Browne's death.

BUT WAIT!
Paul says Tara wasn't the real inspiration and that it was actually inspired by a politician who was on a bunch of drugs at a stoplight, hence the line "He blew his mind out in a car."

What I know now about tripping is you only take a couple and see how you feel. I thought I had to eat a whole dose. I was having insane visuals and audio hallucinations. I just remember the curtains were paisley and the patterns were moving everywhere. All the things in the background were really jumping out at me. I remember looking at other people's costumes and being completely terrified. I ended up in the room of a friend of mine—his name was Ada. We sat and listened to the Beatles for a while, and when "A Day in the Life" hit me, I was just absolutely blown away. It's just always stuck with me. The orchestration.

I love how simply it starts. There's something mystical about it from the very beginning. It opens with the piano and then it swells and it swells. It's the peak of audio engineering and the peak of some of the best songwriting as well. All of that coming together and that being the final track on *Sgt. Pepper*. It's such an amazing way to end an album.

I love the fact that it was written from a true story that John had read in the paper. People read less and less now. It's so romantic to hear John was reading a newspaper. Now it's like, "Oh, I read this on the internet the other day."

What's so cool is that everyone played their part— even the drum parts—they play to the lyrics. Even on that little part, the little interlude that McCartney wrote, "Found my coat and grabbed my hat," and the way the drums take . . . they're playing the music to the lyrics. It makes you feel frantic for a second. We went into a dream and it gets so surreal and dreamy.

There's something about that, when I hear the count off to the song, it's a perfect mix of realism and surrealism. It starts with you reading the news. You don't know if someone's killed themselves, but someone's died. Then it's like, "He blew his mind out in a car" and you realize, "Oh, he's committed suicide." Then everything swells and everything changes! It's not just a song. It's a complete

78

album in one song. It just makes the hair on my arms stand up. I get chills all over my body. My mind was absolutely blown on mushrooms as a nineteen-, twenty-year-old. I didn't know what hit me.

I believe in the afterlife and reincarnation. I definitely believe that this is not all there is. It's easy to get caught up in the now of everything. If something goes wrong, it's such a huge deal. I remind myself that we're all going to die someday and this is just a passing moment. This could be just a dream, you know? I believe that all time is happening at once. I don't know that we can say time only goes forward.

HOLD UP, THOUGH. IS THERE A CONSPIRACY THEORY ABOUT "A DAY IN THE LIFE"?

Sort of! One of the greatest pop culture hoaxes is the "Paul Is Dead" theory that gained steam in 1969 when the student newspaper of Drake University in Des Moines, Iowa, published a lengthy recap of all the clues showing that supposedly Paul McCartney had died in an auto accident years ago and the new Paul was just a fill-in. There were tons of clues that Beatles fans pointed to: the barefoot McCartney on the cover of *Abbey Road*; the spoken message "I buried Paul" by Lennon in "Strawberry Fields Forever," if you played it *backward*; if you played "A Day in the Life" backward, apparently John says, "Paul is dead, miss him, miss him." And of course, the original lyric of blowing his mind out in a car— that was widely interpreted as being about Paul.

MARGO PRICE

In 2018, Margo Price received a Grammy nomination for Best New Artist coming off the heels of her sophomore album, *All American Made*. She's recorded with Willie Nelson and Jack White and performed with legends such as John Prine and Loretta Lynn.

79

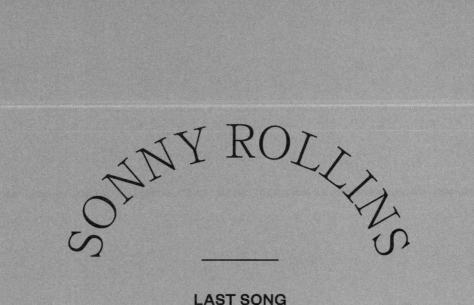

SONNY ROLLINS

LAST SONG

"The Man I Love"

BY COLEMAN HAWKINS (1944)

BECAUSE OF HEALTH PROBLEMS, I haven't performed in years. It took me a little while to accept that I couldn't pick up my saxophone and play it. Playing the sax had been 95 percent of my life. So after dealing with that and coming to terms with it and accepting it, I've begun to write down ideas. There's always music on my mind. I'm never that far away from music.

SONNY ROLLINS

A giant of the classic jazz era of the 1950s and 1960s, saxophonist Sonny Rollins has recorded and performed with legends such as Miles Davis, Thelonious Monk, and John Coltrane. In 2011, President Barack Obama awarded him the National Medal of Arts, alongside Harper Lee, James Taylor, and Meryl Streep.

The first time I really heard Coleman Hawkins was in 1939 with "Body and Soul." Which would be a song I could almost say I'd like to hear as my last song. In fact, there's a friend of mine, he's got one of these rolodexes of music—it wasn't that long ago, I asked him to play some Coleman Hawkins and he played "Body and Soul"—after I heard it, I made the comment, "I've just died and went to heaven." And I meant it. Anything of that nature—any of these songs would be great exit songs from this world.

I had the great pleasure and honor of playing and performing with Coleman Hawkins. Like many of the great artists I had the opportunity to work with, very few of them gave us directions about what to play. No "Do this, do that." They just assumed that if you were up there on the stage playing with them, that you should know what to do. When I played with Miles—Miles would never tell me what to do. Because if you were there, you clearly already knew what to do. And what you did was your signature. If you didn't cut it, you wouldn't be in that particular company. So guys usually don't tell you what to do—not when it comes to improvisation. I remember playing with Monk when he was rehearsing music, and a lot of the guys said, "Hey, Monk, we can't play this music, what is this? These jumps you have!" By the time the rehearsal was over, everybody was playing it and all was well. When it came to improvisation, everybody was left alone.

So I was never nervous when I played with some of my idols. But when I first played with Coleman? I was nervous. I was on my p's and q's in a way that I probably wouldn't be with other people. I was very careful that what I played would be somehow suitable to what he was doing. What the relationship would be in music between him and me. With Coleman I had more of an awareness of what he was going to play—and that what I wanted to play would have some relationship to what he was doing.

We made a record together in 1963, *Sonny Meets Hawk!*, and approached it that way. I knew Coleman Hawkins was a very astute guy. He likes any kind of music and he didn't want to be categorized or periodized. I wanted to do something that was sort of different from exactly playing close to him, in that way, you know. That was my idea. I was very much thinking about playing with him.

If I had to pick my last song, it would be Hawkins's "The Man I Love." It's just a great solo by everybody. I think I'd feel happy and it's the essence of jazz improvisation.

"The Man I Love"

ARTIST
Coleman Hawkins

ORIGINAL COMPOSERS
George and Ira Gershwin

WRITTEN IN
1924, first recorded in 1927

IS THIS SONG ABOUT DEATH?
"The Man I Love" is about finding your Prince Charming. But the song itself nearly died many times. Let me explain. This song was originally slated to be a part of the Gershwins' 1924 production *Lady, Be Good*, but it got dropped. The show was running too long, so something had to be cut. "The Man I Love" was it. The Gershwins decided it would be in 1927's *Strike Up the Band*—but that show never took off. It was included and cut in another show a year later, *Rosalie*. The song finally found life when a handful of musicians started singing it in the late twenties—not long before Sonny Rollins was born.

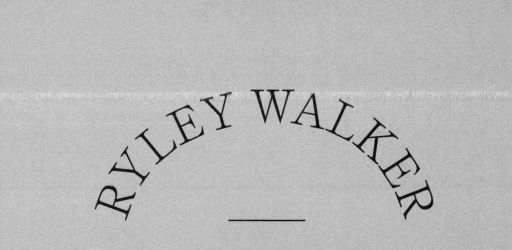

RYLEY WALKER

LAST SONG

"*A Year in a Minute*"

BY FENNESZ (2001)

T HE LAST SONG I'D EVER LISTEN TO IS by Fennesz, the electronic artist. It's called "A Year in a Minute." It's from this record called *Endless Summer*. Don't forget, though: the Beach Boys also have a record called *Endless Summer*, but Fennesz's is exactly the opposite of the Beach Boys'. It's guitars and a bunch of processors, oscillators, and effects pedals. A wall of sound; beautiful, experimental sound. "A Year in a Minute" defined my life for about five years and still does. This whole idea of out-of-body experiences with music—of which I have a lot, some on drugs, some not on drugs—this song is those drugs synthesized into music.

RYLEY WALKER

Ryley Walker is a celebrated guitarist with a prolific streak. He's released several acclaimed albums of classic-folk-inspired music for legendary indie labels Dead Oceans and Thrill Jockey.

When I was nineteen years old, I was getting really into experimental music, drone music. Avant-garde shit. And I remember exactly when I found this album. I went to Reckless Records on Milwaukee Avenue in Chicago. *Endless Summer* was in the dollar bin. I heard this song and it was just pure bliss. And the song title, "A Year in a Minute," it's just so beautiful itself. The song is short, yet listening to it, I feel like I can experience twenty lifetimes. I really mean that. I'm not speaking hyperbole. It's just a perfect song and makes me have nostalgic memories. Jumping over a fence and breaking my arm. Being in fifth grade and shooting a three-pointer into my basketball hoop.

I took LSD with my roommate and we put this song on. It was coming out of one of those iPod docks. He was like, "What is that?" And "Can we listen to that again?" We listened to it for four hours straight, over and over. The song is so dense. It carves out a new path every time I hear it. Which is the beauty about songs you love. Even a song like "Gimme Shelter" by the Rolling Stones, which is my favorite rock song ever. I hear something new every time. This song is a path that dissects my whole life. It bridges every memory into this flowing motion, this mist of the universe. It's the most beautiful song I know. It conjures up good feelings and a weightless, out-of-body sensation.

That's the power of music. It's definitely strange. There are records I can't listen to anymore because of the painful nostalgia they conjure. *It's a Shame About Ray* by the Lemonheads, I can't listen to anymore. Even though it's a happy record, it evokes too many memories of when I was in high school, free, and happy. But there are memories of being sixteen years old and my friend Bob dying. That was his favorite record. So I can't listen to that without thinking of Bob. About a year ago, someone put on *It's a Shame About Ray* and I was like, "Can you please turn this off?"

86

In general, I'm a happy person now. I think I have a pretty good balance in life. I've come around a lot, I've learned a lot. I've done a lot of self-care, a lot of meditation. Therapeutic things, personally and professionally. That's the power that music has. It's too powerful. It's the most powerful shit in the world. It's a hard blast. It's harsher than any cocaine up your nose. It burns.

"A Year in a Minute"

ARTIST
Fennesz

ALBUM
Endless Summer

LENGTH
6 minutes, 4 seconds

WHERE WOULD BE THE BEST PLACE TO LISTEN TO *ENDLESS SUMMER*: HEAVEN, HELL, OR PURGATORY?

This is a great purgatory record. Here's why: the music is very droney and there are a lot of circular motions and acoustic sounds and watery sounds present throughout. Sometimes it's hard to listen to. Sometimes it's easy. You're floating. You're falling. You're dreaming. You're not. That's what this album is and that's what "A Year in a Minute" is. And that's what purgatory is. If purgatory is real and we're going to be trapped there, waiting, there's something about this album that would make it a necessary complement to eternity.

THE MOST
MORBID
NUMBER ONE
SONGS OF
ALL TIME

IN AUGUST 1958, *BILLBOARD* PREMIERED THE Billboard Hot 100 Chart, which originally ranked songs by sales, jukebox spins, and radio plays; in this century, the weekly list blends sales, streams, and airplay data.

Looking back on sixty-plus years of number one hits, a few things stand out.

Love rules. There are millions of songs written about love and it seems that this topic, above anything else, can make for a massive hit.

Oh, and also sex. Sex sells, and people like to listen to musicians sing about sex. This was especially prevalent in the 1990s and early 2000s. Coming in a close second during that time frame was "the club." Everyone loved going to the club, dancing in the club, just being in the club in general.

Which brings us to death. Death typically doesn't make for a great topic with which to top the charts. But surprisingly, there have been numerous songs to reach the top of the *Billboard* Hot 100 that are quite morbid. And some lasted for *weeks*.

Here's a snapshot of each decade the Hot 100 has been active and what morbid songs topped the charts.

1950s

1959

"Stagger Lee"

ARTIST
Lloyd Price

WEEKS AT NO. 1
Four (Feb. 9–March 2)

SAMPLE LYRIC
"'Stagger Lee,' cried Billy / 'Oh, please don't take my life / I've got three little children and a very sickly wife' / Stagger Lee shot Billy / Oh, he shot that poor boy so bad / Till the bullet came through Billy / And it broke the bartender's glass."

TYPE OF DEATH
Murder

"Mack the Knife"

ARTIST
Bobby Darin

WEEKS AT NO. 1
Nine (Oct. 5–Nov. 9; Nov. 23–Dec. 7)

SAMPLE LYRIC
Now, on the sidewalk, ooh Sunday morning / Lies a body just oozing life / And someone's sneaking around the corner / Could that be Mack the Knife?"

TYPE OF DEATH
Murder

1960s

1960

"El Paso"

ARTIST
Marty Robbins

WEEKS AT NO. 1
Two (Jan. 4–11)

SAMPLE LYRIC
"Quickly she grabbed for the six-gun that he wore / And screamin' in anger and placin' the gun to her breast / Bury us both deep and maybe we'll find peace / And pullin' the trigger, she fell 'cross the dead cow boy's chest."

TYPE OF DEATH
Suicide by gunshot

"Running Bear"

ARTIST
Johnny Preston

WEEKS AT NO. 1
Three (Jan. 18–Feb. 1)

SAMPLE LYRIC
"Running Bear dove in the water / Little White Dove did the same / And they swam out to each other / Through the swirling stream they came / As their hands touched and their lips met / The raging river pulled them down / Now they'll always be together / In their happy hunting ground."

TYPE OF DEATH
Joint suicide by drowning

"Teen Angel"

ARTIST
Mark Dinning

WEEKS AT NO. 1
Two (Feb. 8–Feb. 15)

SAMPLE LYRIC
"That fateful night the car was stalled / Upon the railroad track / I pulled you out and we were safe / But you went running back / . . . What was it you were looking for / That took your life that night / They said they found my high school ring / Clutched in your fingers tight."

TYPE OF DEATH
Hit by a train

1961

"Moody River"

ARTIST
Pat Boone

WEEKS AT NO. 1
One (June 19)

SAMPLE LYRIC
"Moody river more deadly / Than the vainest knife / Moody river your muddy water / Took my baby's life."

TYPE OF DEATH
Suicide by drowning

"Big Bad John"

ARTIST
Jimmy Dean

WEEKS AT NO. 1
Five (Nov. 6–Dec. 4)

SAMPLE LYRIC
"With jacks and timbers they started back down / Then came that rumble way down in the ground / And then smoke and gas belched out of that mine / Everybody knew it was the end of the line for Big John."

TYPE OF DEATH
Unfortunate mining accident

1964

"Leader of the Pack"

ARTIST
The Shangri-Las

WEEKS AT NO. 1
One (Nov. 28)

SAMPLE LYRIC
"I felt so helpless, what could I do? / Remembering all the things we'd been through / In school they all stop and stare / I can't hide the tears, but I don't care / I'll never forget him, the leader of the pack."

TYPE OF DEATH
Motorcycle crash

"Ringo"

ARTIST
Lorne Greene

WEEKS AT NO. 1
One (Dec. 5)

SAMPLE LYRIC
"I blocked the path of his retreat / He turned and stepped into the street / A dozen guns spit fire and lead / A moment later, he lay dead / The town began to shout and cheer / Nowhere was there shed a tear for Ringo."

TYPE OF DEATH
Gunfire by an angry mob

1965

"Eve of Destruction"

ARTIST
Barry McGuire

WEEKS AT NO. 1
One (Sept. 25)

SAMPLE LYRIC
"The eastern world, it is explodin' / Violence flarin', bullets loadin' / You're old enough to kill but not for votin' / You don't believe in war, what's that gun you're totin' / And even the Jordan river has bodies floatin' / But you tell me over and over and over again my friend / Ah, you don't believe we're on the eve of destruction."

TYPE OF DEATH
The horrors of war

1966

"The Ballad of the Green Berets"

ARTIST
SSgt. Barry Sadler

WEEKS AT NO. 1
Five (March 5–April 2)

SAMPLE LYRIC
"Back at home a young wife waits / Her Green Beret has met his fate / He has died for those oppressed / Leaving her his last request / Put silver wings on my son's chest / Make him one of America's best / He'll be a man they'll test one day / Have him win the Green Beret."

TYPE OF DEATH
War

"Paint It Black"

ARTIST
The Rolling Stones

WEEKS AT NO. 1
Two (June 11–18)

SAMPLE LYRIC
"I see a line of cars and they're all painted black / With flowers and my love both never to come back / I see people turn their heads and quickly look away / Like a newborn baby it just happens every day."

TYPE OF DEATH
Unknown

1967

"Ode to Billie Joe"

ARTIST
Bobbie Gentry

WEEKS AT NO. 1
Four (Aug. 26–Sept. 16)

SAMPLE LYRIC
"There's five more acres in the lower forty I've got to plow / And Mama said it was shame about Billy Joe, anyhow / Seems like nothin' ever comes to no good up on Choctaw Ridge / And now Billie Joe McAllister's jumped off the Tallahatchie Bridge."

TYPE OF DEATH
Suicide

1968

"Honey"

ARTIST
Bobby Goldsboro

WEEKS AT NO. 1
Five (April 13–May 11)

SAMPLE LYRIC
"One day while I was not at home / While she was there and all alone / The angels came / Now all I have is memories of Honey / And I wake up nights and call her name."

TYPE OF DEATH
Unknown

1969

"In the Year 2525"

ARTIST
Zager & Evans

WEEKS AT NO. 1
Six (July 12–Aug. 16)

SAMPLE LYRIC
"In the year 8510 / God is gonna shake His mighty head / He'll either say, 'I'm pleased where man has been' / Or tear it down and start again."

TYPE OF DEATH
The complete demise of humanity

1970s

1972

"American Pie"

ARTIST
Don McLean

WEEKS AT NO. 1
Four (Jan. 15–Feb. 5)

SAMPLE LYRIC
"Bye, bye, Miss American Pie / Drove my Chevy to the levee, but the levee was dry / And them good ole boys were drinking whiskey 'n rye / Singing, 'This'll be the day that I die / This'll be the day that I die.'"

TYPE OF DEATH
Plane crash—the song was infamously inspired by the day the Big Bopper, Buddy Holly, and Ritchie Valens died, on February 3, 1959. "American Pie" dubbed this "The day the music died."

"Alone Again (Naturally)"

ARTIST
Gilbert O'Sullivan

WEEKS AT NO. 1
Six (July 29–Aug. 19; Sept. 2–9)

SAMPLE LYRIC
"In a little while from now / If I'm not feeling any less sour / I promise myself to treat myself / And visit a nearby tower / And climbing to the top / Will throw myself off / In an effort to make it clear to whoever / What it's like when you're shattered."

TYPE OF DEATH
Threatening suicide, plus parents' death

"Papa Was a Rollin' Stone"

ARTIST
The Temptations

WEEKS AT NO. 1
One (Dec. 2)

SAMPLE LYRIC
"It was the third of September / That day I'll always remember, yes I will / 'Cause that was the day that my daddy died / I never got a chance to see him / Never heard nothin' but bad things about him.

TYPE OF DEATH
Unknown; the song details an absentee father who finally died, leaving his family to fend for themselves.

1973

"The Night the Lights Went Out in Georgia"

ARTIST
Vicki Lawrence

WEEKS AT NO. 1
Two (April 7–14)

SAMPLE LYRIC
"Well, they hung my brother before I could say / The tracks he saw while on his way / To Andy's house and back that night were mine / And his cheating wife had never left town / And that's one body that'll never be found / See, little sister don't miss when she aims her gun."

TYPE OF DEATH
Murder by gunshot + execution by hanging

1974

"Seasons in the Sun"

ARTIST
Terry Jacks

WEEKS AT NO. 1
Three (March 2–16)

SAMPLE LYRIC
"Goodbye my friend, it's hard to die / When all the birds are singing in the sky / Now that the spring is in the air / Pretty girls are everywhere / Think of me and I'll be there."

TYPE OF DEATH
Unknown; someone on their deathbed

"Dark Lady"

ARTIST
Cher

WEEKS AT NO. 1
One (March 23)

SAMPLE LYRIC
"So I snuck back and caught her with my man / Laughing and kissing till they saw the gun in my hand / The next thing I knew they were dead on the floor / Dark Lady would never turn a card up anymore."

TYPE OF DEATH
Double murder

"Billy, Don't Be a Hero"

ARTIST
Bo Donaldson and the Heywoods

WEEKS AT NO. 1
Two (June 15–22)

SAMPLE LYRIC
"I heard his fiancée got a letter / That told how Billy died that day / The letter said that he was a hero / She should be proud he died that way."

TYPE OF DEATH
War

"The Night Chicago Died"

ARTIST
Paper Lace

WEEKS AT NO. 1
One (Aug. 17)

SAMPLE LYRIC
"There was shouting in the street / And the sound of running feet / And I asked someone who said / "Bout a hundred cops are dead!"

TYPE OF DEATH
Gang wars

"I Shot the Sheriff"

ARTIST
Eric Clapton

WEEKS AT NO. 1
One (Sept. 14)

SAMPLE LYRIC
"I shot the sheriff, but I did not shoot the deputy."

TYPE OF DEATH
Murder

1980s

1980

"Another One Bites the Dust"

ARTIST
Queen

WEEKS AT NO. 1
Three (Oct. 4–18)

SAMPLE LYRIC
"Are you ready? Hey, are you ready for this? / Are you standing on the edge of your seat? / Out of the doorway the bullets rip / To the sound of the beat / Another one bites the dust."

TYPE OF DEATH
Gang shootout

1981

"Rapture"

ARTIST
Blondie

WEEKS AT NO. 1
Two (March 28–April 4)

SAMPLE LYRIC
"And out comes the man from Mars / And you try to run but he's got a gun / And he shoots you dead and he eats your head / And then you're in the man from Mars."

TYPE OF DEATH
The Apocalypse

1985

"A View to a Kill"

ARTIST
Duran Duran

WEEKS AT NO. 1
Two (July 13–20)

SAMPLE LYRIC
"The choice for you is the view to a kill / Between the shades assassination standing still."

TYPE OF DEATH
It's an ode to an assassin.

1988

"Man in the Mirror"

ARTIST
Michael Jackson

WEEKS AT NO. 1
Two (March 26–April 2)

SAMPLE LYRIC
N/A

TYPE OF DEATH
While the song isn't morbid, per se, Jackson dedicated the tune to a young Japanese boy who was abducted and murdered. On the record's sleeve, there's a note that says, "May such a terrible thing never happen again. I will always love you. —Michael Jackson."

1989

"The Living Years"

ARTIST
Mike + The Mechanics

WEEKS AT NO. 1
One (March 25)

SAMPLE LYRIC
"I wasn't there that morning / When my father passed away / I didn't get to tell him / All the things I had to say / I think I caught his spirit / Later that same year / I'm sure I heard his echo / In my baby's newborn tears / I just wish I could have told him in the living years."

TYPE OF DEATH
A father's passing

"Eternal Flame"

ARTIST
The Bangles

WEEKS AT NO. 1
One (April 1)

SAMPLE LYRIC
N/A

TYPE OF DEATH
No death referenced in the song, but it was inspired by a trip Susanna Hoffs took to Elvis Presley's grave site, where a flame burns 24/7.

1990s

1990

"Blaze of Glory"

ARTIST
Jon Bon Jovi

WEEKS AT NO. 1
One (Sept. 8)

SAMPLE LYRIC
"Lord, I gotta ask a favor, and I hope you'll understand / 'Cause I've lived life to the fullest, let this boy die like a man / Starin' down a bullet, let me make my final stand."

TYPE OF DEATH
A shootout

1995

"Waterfalls"

ARTIST
TLC

WEEKS AT NO. 1
Seven (July 8–Aug. 19)

SAMPLE LYRIC
"One day he goes and takes a glimpse in the mirror / But he doesn't recognize his own face / His health is fading and he doesn't know why / Three letters took him to his final resting place."

TYPE OF DEATH
HIV/AIDS

1996

"Tha Crossroads"

ARTIST
Bone Thugs-N-Harmony

WEEKS AT NO. 1
Eight (May 18–July 6)

SAMPLE LYRIC
"Can somebody anybody tell me why? / Hey, can somebody anybody tell me why? / We die, we die? / I don't wanna die."

TYPE OF DEATH
A friend's untimely death

1997

"I'll Be Missing You"

ARTIST
Puff Daddy and Faith Evans, featuring 112

WEEKS AT NO. 1
Eleven (June 14–Aug. 23)

SAMPLE LYRIC
"Life ain't always what it seem to be / Words can't express what you mean to me / Even though you're gone, we still a team / Through your family, I'll fulfill your dream."

TYPE OF DEATH
It's also a tribute song, to the Notorious B.I.G., who had been shot and killed.

1997–1998

"Candle in the Wind 1997 / Something About the Way You Look Tonight"

ARTIST
Elton John

WEEKS AT NO. 1
Fourteen (Oct. 11, 1997–Jan. 10, 1998)

SAMPLE LYRIC
"Goodbye England's rose / May you ever grow in our hearts / You were the grace that placed itself / Where lives were torn apart."

TYPE OF DEATH
It's a tribute to Princess Diana, written after her death.

1998

"Together Again"

ARTIST
Janet Jackson

WEEKS AT NO. 1
Two (Jan. 31–Feb. 7)

SAMPLE LYRIC
"What I'd give just to hold you close as on earth / In heaven, we will be together, baby / Together again, my baby."

TYPE OF DEATH
The song was inspired by losing a friend to AIDS-related complications.

2000s

2004

"Slow Motion"

ARTIST
Juvenile feat. Soulja Slim

WEEKS AT NO. 1
Two (Aug. 7–14)

SAMPLE LYRIC
N/A

TYPE OF DEATH
The song came out after Soulja Slim was murdered in November 2003, the video had "RIP Soulja" shirts on display and signs that read "Thou Shall Not Kill."

2007

"Beautiful Girls"

ARTIST
Sean Kingston

WEEKS AT NO. 1
Four (Aug. 11–Sept. 1)

SAMPLE LYRIC
"You're way too beautiful, girl / That's why it'll never work / You'll have me suicidal, suicidal / When you say it's over."

TYPE OF DEATH
Suicide. Even though the lines are metaphorical, radio stations played an alternate version so it wouldn't encourage people to kill themselves.

2009

"Crack a Bottle"

ARTIST
Eminem, Dr. Dre, and 50 Cent

WEEKS AT NO. 1
One (Feb. 21)

SAMPLE LYRIC
"Ladies and gentlemen / The moment you've all been waiting for / In this corner, weighing 175 pounds / With a record of 17 rapes, 400 assaults, and 4 murders / The undisputed, most diabolical villain in the world / Slim Shady.

TYPE OF DEATH
Not a death, per se, but in this song the artist says he's a rapist and a murderer. Sarcastically, of course. But still.

2010s

2010

"We R Who We R"

ARTIST
Kesha

WEEKS AT NO. 1
One (Nov. 13)

SAMPLE LYRIC
N/A

TYPE OF DEATH
It was a response to a recent wave of teen suicides.

2011

"Grenade"

ARTIST
Bruno Mars

WEEKS AT NO. 1
Four (Jan. 8–22; Feb. 5–12)

SAMPLE LYRIC
"I would go through all this pain / Take a bullet straight through my brain / Yes, I would die for ya, baby / But you won't do the same."

TYPE OF DEATH
Suicide

2015

"See You Again"

ARTIST
Wiz Khalifa featuring Charlie Puth

WEEKS AT NO. 1
Twelve (4/25–5/30; 6/13–7/18)

SAMPLE LYRIC
"It's been a long day without you, my friend / And I'll tell you all about it when I see you again."

TYPE OF DEATH
It's a tribute to *Fast & Furious* star Paul Walker, who died in a car crash in November 2013.

Want to hear these songs in this order? Search "The Most Morbid Billboard No. 1's" in Spotify for the playlist.

ANGEL OLSEN

LAST SONG

"Always It's You"

BY THE EVERLY BROTHERS (1960)

I T WAS REALLY DIFFICULT FOR ME TO FIND just one song. But I have thought about this a lot. Whenever I'm on a plane and it's crazy, it's like, "This could be it!" I try to listen to an upbeat song, like Fleetwood Mac. But I didn't want to pick Fleetwood Mac because I feel like that's such a given, you know?

ANGEL OLSEN

Angel Olsen is a Chicago-based musician who mixes indie pop and rock throughout her records. Her latest album, 2019's *All Mirrors*, landed in the top ten of numerous best-of-the-year lists for various outlets, including Pitchfork, NPR, Stereogum, and the *Guardian*.

When I was maybe twenty-two, twenty-three, I was having a lot of relationship issues with a partner. I was living with three people in this apartment in Chicago's Logan Square, before Logan Square blew up and had baby stores and stuff. And we found out we had bedbugs. It was the middle of the summer, so we thought it was mosquitoes as first.

It was me and three other people and there was a drum set in the middle of the living room. Everybody's kinda hanging out all the time. People are coming over to practice. I used to smoke, so we'd all sit in the backroom and there was a turntable there, and we used to sit and smoke, drink beer, and talk—that was our little zone.

We had this meeting back there one day. And someone was like, "We don't know where it started. But we have bedbugs." We all inspected everyone's stuff and it became this thing where we all, very quickly, could tell who it psychologically damaged and who wasn't taking any precautions at all. My boyfriend at the time was like, "You can't come over. You're going to have to wash your clothes, put them in a bag, put them in the hallway, change in the hallway . . ." I was like, "This is too insane. We can't have sex anymore. I can't be a leper anymore. Just trust that I showered and scrubbed everywhere."

One of the roommates was this guy who was dating a lot of women and not telling them we have bedbugs. We were like, "Dude, Ellie and I are going to take all your things to a laundromat because you're not doing a thing to help the situation. And you need to tell whoever you're dating, they can't come over. We are quarantined to this house. People can't come and visit."

So we were living out of plastic bags. And we drank a lot already, but when this happened, we were stuck in our house, with each other, and we just drank all summer to get through this. But luckily we had a rooftop, so in the late summer, we got a ladder and went up to the rooftop a lot. We put some Astroturf down, got some lawn chairs, and we played a lot of music on the speaker. It was like, "Everyone will be okay. I will have real furniture again and this won't haunt me forever."

Ellie and I would listen to a lot of old music and get high, to alleviate the stress. And it was the first time, this summer, that I remember getting really high and listening to this song by the Everly Brothers on repeat called "Always It's You." Lying on the Astroturf being like, "This is the end. I'm dead now. I have bedbugs in my apartment, my boyfriend is leaving me because I'm a leper, the people at work don't want to talk to me. But this song is saving my life now. And if I were to die listening to it right now, it would be an amazing experience."

I think about death a lot because I'm traveling all the time. I guess it's a thing about getting older. I'm thirty-three as of this writing. I feel like I've calmed down a bit and things don't emotionally affect me the same way. Thinking about death inspires me to do the reverse thing. It lights a fire under my ass to do more shit.

I'm obsessed with the idea, like a song or a recording, the idea that music can be almost like you're living more, by capturing it. You get to share a part of your soul for as long as the recording exists. And that is a spooky, cool thing that I think about a lot. Sound is everything. It's this thing that creates its own architecture in your head. It's part of what makes me want to put more work into my writing. I hope if I put more effort into writing, it's my way of living more.

That summer, because of what happened, I'll always remember it. I'll always remember the first time I heard that song. I listen to a lot of music and it doesn't always affect me that way. But it just really . . . it really hit me. I was really depressed. It's a funny thing to think about now, but I felt so isolated.

"Always It's You"

WRITTEN BY
Felice and Boudleaux Bryant, a husband-and-wife songwriting force. They wrote other massive Everly Brothers hits, such as "Wake Up Little Susie," "Bye Bye Love," and "Rocky Top."

ALBUM
1960's *A Date with the Everly Brothers*

LENGTH
2 minutes, 30 seconds

IS THIS SONG ABOUT DEATH?
Nope. Like nearly every Everly Brothers song, it's about true love.

ADAM GRANDUCIEL

THE WAR ON DRUGS

LAST SONG

"Crying"

BY ROY ORBISON (1961)

I FIRST REMEMBER HEARING ROY ORBISON on my mom's cassette in her car. She had one cassette. My dad had maybe two cassettes in his car: the soundtrack to *Cats* and some classical music. The radio was set to either the classical station or sports radio or Paul Harvey. But in my mom's car there was just a Roy Orbison cassette and that was it. I remember waiting in the car when she would go in and get the eggs from the chicken at the poultry farm and listening to "Crying" and that album.

ADAM GRANDUCIEL

Based out of Philadelphia, Adam Granducial's band the War on Drugs has released four albums and gained a worldwide following over the last fifteen years. The band's 2017 album *A Deeper Understanding* won the Grammy for Best Rock Album.

Orbison in general is one of the first musicians I remember hearing and liking and going back to and asking to hear again. I was like seven or eight, you know? He's been with me my whole life. Musicians all looked at Orbison as the king. And that song is undeniable in its craft. You never get bored with the end when he goes up. You never get bored of the melody. It's a classic, perfect moment. If I had to listen to one thing on a loop for the rest of my life, that would be it.

When I was maybe fourteen or fifteen, I had already gotten super into music just from being a teenager. I found a lot of it on my own. But I remember being at my grandmother's house and finding my mom's records from when she was a kid. And they were always in the bedroom that we put our coats in. The Beatles' *White Album*, the Stones, Clapton's *Crossroads*. All that kinda stuff. It's like, "Oh, I forgot that you're a person, too, or you were my age once, too." Culturally, you're probably made aware of *Sgt. Pepper* when you're four or five. But when you hold it in your hands for the first time, you're like, "Oh wow, this is that thing I kinda know about but never really held or listened to." She didn't have a million incredible records, but any pop record that you would have bought between 1964 and 1968 was pretty much there. I remember being consumed by the question of whether or not she would let me take them out of my grandmother's house and bring them home. I didn't have a record player yet, but I wanted them to be mine.

I think everything I know now about songwriting, everything I'm into now—everything about "Crying" is so simple. The production is probably three mics in a room. The production is so simple, the song is so simple, you can sing it the second time you hear it. But if you're making music for a living, that's the gold standard—simplicity at that level. Usually, my favorite songs, songs that I feel compelled to cover with the band, I gravitate to them because usually there's something so simple and perfect.

At the time I was listening to Roy Orbison, I didn't think I was getting into one of the kings of rock and roll. I just thought I was getting into my mom's tape. But time has proven that he's one of the kings. Looking back now, he was one of the guys who got me into rock and roll. Within six years, I was wearing a Nirvana T-shirt. Roy and Nirvana were my first two favorite things.

That favorite scene of a movie—the first five times you watched it, it blew you away. Now it doesn't really blow you away. You're impressed by it. You know it's there. But a song—put that on in the right moment—and it still floors you. It's simplicity and beauty. And its message. It's a guy who's down and out. He's crying, you know? That's all it is. It's one of those songs that, without me even knowing it, introduced me to rock and roll. And later in life, it set the standard for what I'm trying to do: be simple and to the point.

"Crying"

ARTIST
Roy Orbison

ALBUM
Crying

LENGTH
2 minutes, 46 seconds

CHART POSITION
No. 2 on the Billboard Hot 100

THE "CRYING" COMEBACK
Orbison recorded a duet with k. d. lang, released in 1987, and they won a Grammy for best country collaboration with vocals, about twenty-six years after the original was released. A year later, he would die from a heart attack.

IS THIS SONG ABOUT DEATH?
Breaking up with someone can surely make you feel like you're going to DIE, but at its core, "Crying" is not about death. Just about the age-old tradition of moving on from someone romantically.

"I was dating a girl and we broke up," Orbison told authors Spencer Leigh and Jon Kutner for their book *1,000 UK Number One Hits*. "I went to the barber shop to get a haircut and I looked across the street and there was this girl that I had split up with. I wanted to go over and say, 'Let's forget about what happened and carry on.' But I was stubborn. So I got in the car and drove down the street about two blocks and said to myself, 'Boy, you really made a mistake. You didn't play that right at all.' It certainly brought tears to my eyes and that's how I came up with 'Crying.'"

103

KEVIN MORBY

LAST SONG

"It's All Over Now, Baby Blue"

BY BOB DYLAN (1965)

I HAVE MY FUNERAL SONGS IN MY HEAD and there are definitely three that would need to be played. Bob Dylan's "It's All Over Now, Baby Blue," Leonard Cohen's "Passing Through," and Nina Simone's version of "I Shall Be Released." Those are "the credits are about to roll" sorta songs. And they're just so beautiful, but they're also very sad. There's something very somber about them. They all encompass life and are about the beginning and ending of things. So I knew it would have to be one of those songs.

KEVIN MORBY

Kevin Morby is a Kansas-based singer-songwriter. He started his musical career in the psychedelic indie-rock band Woods, and his latest album is 2019's *Oh My God*.

But I feel like the Leonard Cohen song and the Nina Simone song—those are songs that need to play while the credits *actually* roll. Whereas "It's All Over Now, Baby Blue"—that's more of a song that's the last scene of a movie, the last part of someone's life. There's something a little sinister about that song. It's beautiful, but it's not all beautiful. The beauty can set in once you're actually dead or passed on. He's describing characters and these moods he's gone through. In the way of a last meal, if I was on death row, and they brought in a last song, and they gave me a tape and it had "It's All Over Now, Baby Blue," I could really get a montage of my life. So I think that's the song.

The first time I heard it was when I was probably seventeen. I was in my bedroom in Kansas City, and it was around Christmastime. I got really into Bob Dylan when I was fourteen or fifteen, and I was really into those first three records. The super-folkie stuff where it was just him and a guitar. In getting more into the world of him, the first electric Dylan record I ever got was *Bringing It All Back Home*. I think what turned me on to that record was seeing the Pennebaker documentary *Dont Look Back*, the one that starts off with "Subterranean Homesick Blues." I got the record and I remember putting it on and not loving the A side. I was like, "This is cool, but not as good as his acoustic stuff." But then I put on the B side, which has "Mr. Tambourine Man." And when "It's Alright, Ma (I'm Only Bleeding)" came on—I couldn't believe how good a song that was. It just seemed like time stopped. I couldn't believe that somebody had written poetry as perfect as that. The record was spinning and I couldn't stop looking at the lyrics. I thought that had to be the last song, a song that good. But that song ends and "It's All Over Now, Baby Blue" came on and I was like, "This song is better!" It kinda blew my mind.

To me, it's so much about death. The saints are coming in. The vagabonds are rapping on the door. It's a person at the end of something, looking back on something. That's why I used the word *sinister*. There's something about "I Shall Be Released" or "Passing Through" that's almost like "I was happy to be here." There's a tone in "It's All Over Now, Baby Blue" that's like "I never asked to be here." Like, this wasn't all perfect.

I think he was writing that song at the end of a part of his career: the acoustic part of his career and starting to see a lot of cynicism and change in the Greenwich Village scene. But it's obviously a song about something ending and that's why I think it's perfect.

"It's All Over Now, Baby Blue"

ARTIST
Bob Dylan

RECORDED ON
January 15, 1965

ALBUM
Bringing It All Back Home

LENGTH
4 minutes, 12 seconds

THEORIES ABOUT WHO BABY BLUE IS

Joan Baez—they were about to break up

David Blue—a Greenwich Village folk singer Dylan was friends with

Paul Clayton—another folk singer friend with whom Dylan seemingly got annoyed

The Acoustic Life—the notion that Dylan was moving on to the electric phase of his career

His folk audience—at the infamous Newport Folk Festival in 1965, where he got booed for going electric—the last song of his acoustic set was in fact "It's All Over Now, Baby Blue"

ARTISTS' COVERS INCLUDE
Van Morrison, the Animals, the Grateful Dead, the 13th Floor Elevators, Marianne Faithfull, Echo & the Bunnymen, Matthew Sweet and Susanna Hoffs, Bryan Ferry, Bad Religion, the Byrds, and Joan Baez(!)

KEVIN MORBY

WILL OLDHAM

IF THERE WAS A SONG I'D DIE TO RIGHT
at this moment, it's different from if I'm eighty-five years
old and dying of cancer, or eighty-nine years old in the
advanced stages of Alzheimer's. Or fifty-five years old at a
ski lodge in the Swiss Alps. I'd listen to something in my ski
lodge, put on my skis and hit the slopes, and then go run into
a tree. They would all be different songs, right?

One of the first things I thought was, if you had just said "in general" when you posed the question—as "in general your existence is about to end"—I'm not sure I would prioritize a commercial recording. If I was given ten possible things to choose from that would be my last sensory experience, I'm not sure I would be like, "I'll just get my Spotify playlist, it's all going to end!" I might think of a smell or a touch or somebody's voice singing a song. It feels strange knowing that everything we are talking about might be a commercial product on some level. I have such deep connections to lots of pieces of music, but when it comes right down to it, is that the thing I want reverberating in my brain when they freeze-frame my last moment of consciousness? I don't know.

The thing I like about my own recordings is that they bring up memories of other musicians I've played with. As valuable as those relationships and experiences are, there are things and people that I would put above those wonderful memories. And knowing how loaded those are for me, I know when I'm listening to anybody's music, those songs have the potential to be as loaded for those artists.

I listen to a lot of Cat Stevens. I've listened to all the records he's made in the last ten years—he's always addressing grand themes in big ways and small, and making them idiosyncratic and beautiful. But I think if someone was like, "Okay, it's your last three minutes and forty-eight seconds," I'd be like, "Oh, get these earbuds out! I want to hang out right here with my wife and baby. Turn the music off! Somebody turn that music off!"

I know that, at this point, especially those of us who work in music, we contain so much music. I could listen to Lou Reed's "Perfect Day" or "Street Hassle." Most of the nuances of those songs I have inside of me. People say, "You know how you see your life flash in front of you?" I could probably listen to one of those whole songs in a fraction of a second and listen to a whole other five songs in a fraction of a second, where it skips on my copy of that record. *It's just in me.*

And that's the same for my own music. More than other people's music, I learn more about it the more I listen to it. If someone would say, "Something is going to happen and your existence is going to end in a month and you have to listen to some music," I'd probably say, "Okay, let's make a new record." The new record will just be my wife and daughter and a bunch of my friends coming in to sing on all the choruses. Have that experience. Something that's happening as opposed to something that has already happened. So if my moment was a solitary one or a lonely one, I'd have that as a reminder of everything.

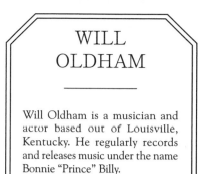

WILL
OLDHAM

Will Oldham is a musician and actor based out of Louisville, Kentucky. He regularly records and releases music under the name Bonnie "Prince" Billy.

111

JULIA HOLTER

LAST SONG

"*Yamuna
Tira Vihari*"

BY ALICE COLTRANE (1982)

Julia Holter is a Los Angeles–based musician whose work constantly pushes conventional notions about song structure and composition. She's toured extensively throughout North America and Europe and performed at major music festivals such as Pitchfork Festival, Sasquatch, and Primavera Sound.

W HEN I FIRST HEARD THE song "Yamuna Tira Vihari" by Alice Coltrane, I was at this show I did with this internet radio station based out of LA called Dublab. Mark McNeill from Dublab—"DJ Frosty"—was playing this track. It was this thing called *Tonalism* that the radio station does, an all-night music show.

We were in Toronto, in this church, and I wanted a quick nap; it was around 4:30 or 5:00 in the morning. So I fell asleep on this hardwood pew after being awake all night. I was super delirious. When I woke up, this music was playing. And I had never really heard Alice before, but it was a very important musical moment for me. It was a little bit spiritual, but not in a religious way.

The album it's from is called *Turiya Sings*, and it was released in 1982. It's described as "Devotional Songs in Original Composition with Organ and Strings." These are sacred songs. Alice's voice was echoing through the church, and it was a low voice, chanting. It felt like the most beautiful music . . . some of the most useful music I've ever heard. The strings merged with a synthesizer, producing a gliding sensation. Harmonically, timberly, melodically—it was just so beautiful.

This record has become very important to me, especially in difficult times. I just listen to it and it's calming. You immediately see the beauty in everything. I don't know how else to explain it. It's really cathartic for me. It grounds me in a way, and lifts me at the same time. I feel like a creature sharing with the world. I don't know. It does everything. For me, it feels very essential.

There's a blanket of organ and then a voice that comes over the top and is lulling. So, it's calming and puts things in perspective in a way. Things are still, but also vibrating. Which is kind of how things are! That's what the world is. It only seems still.

When we're doing all our things every day, we're moving everything around. I'm moving this chair, I'm walking my body around. Cars are driving by. Everything is either completely still and motionless or we're pushing it. The reality is that everything is constantly moving. I think it's the Heisenberg uncertainty principle or something? It's like that kind of thing. I'm being a little abstractive and hippie—but it is true! It's all moving. You can't actually measure where an object is in time. It was true when I was in high school, in chemistry class. I still think about it. That's what that song does. It reminds me that everything exists. And that would be a good way to go out.

"Yamuna Tira Vihari"

YEAR RELEASED
1982

ALBUM
Turiya Sings

LENGTH
6 minutes, 8 seconds

IS THIS SONG ABOUT DEATH?
This song is likely about life. But who knows! It certainly has an interesting backstory. Alice Coltrane, who was married to John Coltrane, left the world of making secular music to start the Shanti Anantam Ashram outside of Los Angeles. It was a Hindu community on a forty-eight-acre plot of land. While there, unbeknownst to the larger world, she recorded a number of spiritual albums, beginning with *Turiya Sings*. She gave them out to the devotees at the ashram on cassette tape—there was no commercial intention; just music for music's sake; prayer and meditation for prayer and meditation's sake. There are no reviews or interviews about it.

Coltrane devoted herself to Vedanta, the most prominent of the six ancient Hindu philosophies. In Vedanta, they believe in rebirth. And knowing that and listening to "Yamuna Tira Vihari," a song with lyrics that describe Madhava Hari on the banks of a river playing a flute, you can easily make the leap that this is a song about life and death and circles and everything surrounding us.

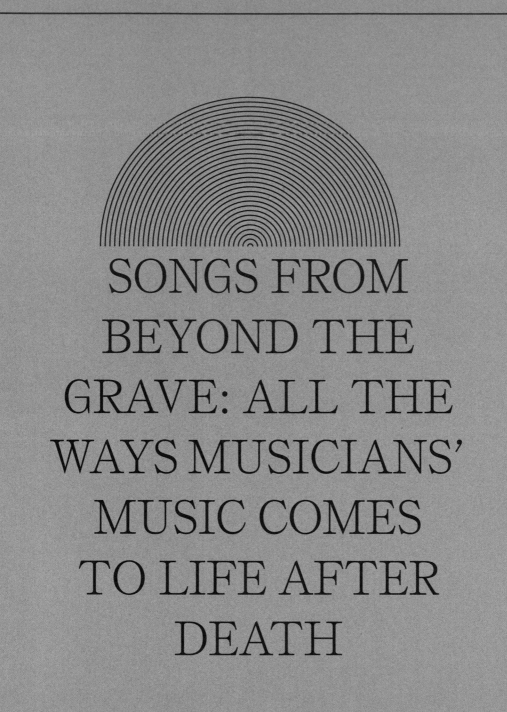

SONGS FROM BEYOND THE GRAVE: ALL THE WAYS MUSICIANS' MUSIC COMES TO LIFE AFTER DEATH

J UST BECAUSE YOU'RE DEAD DOESN'T MEAN you can't still make a meaningful musical contribution and a boatload of cash for your loved ones (or whoever owns the rights to your catalog).

Is this a good thing? A bad thing? Here are nine ways musicians' music came to life after death—and the crazy things that can happen.

YOU CAN FINALLY HIT NUMBER ONE

When David Bowie died on January 10, 2016, he had never had a number one album in the US. But that would change immediately in the wake of his passing. *Blackstar*, his twenty-fifth and final studio album (released just two days before he died, on January 8), hit number one on the *Billboard* 200 the following week.

YOU CAN WIN PRESTIGIOUS ADVERTISING AWARDS

In April 2012, a Tupac hologram "performed" at Coachella with Dr. Dre and Snoop Dogg, setting off debates about legacy, artistic desires, and resting in peace. The Tupac Hologram went on to win the Titanium Award at the Cannes Lions International Festival of Creativity two months later. According to a press release at the time, this award "recognizes the most groundbreaking work in the creative communications field" and "Virtual 2Pac" was chosen by an "elite" panel of ten jurors.

YOU CAN RECORD WITH ORCHESTRAS

In 2015, Elvis Presley released *If I Can Dream*, a record with the Royal Philharmonic Orchestra, in which his vocals were mixed with new recordings from the famed classical group. The album went to number one in the UK and Australia.

YOU CAN REPEAT CHART HISTORY

Michael Jackson returned to the charts in 2014 with a new song, "Love Never Felt So Good," a duet with Justin Timberlake. Jackson's vocals were taken from an '83 demo and the song entered the Billboard Hot 100 charts at number 20—the same opening spot "Thriller" took thirty years prior.

YOU CAN WIN MULTIPLE GRAMMYS

Nat King Cole's iconic song "Unforgettable" returned to pop-culture prominence twenty-six years after he died. In this instance, his daughter Natalie recorded a version that spliced her vocals with her father's. And EVERYONE lapped it up . . . making it pretty un . . . for . . . gettable. (Sorry.) It won two Grammys in 1992: Record of the Year and Best Traditional Pop Vocal Performance.

YOU CAN SPEAK FROM BEYOND THE GRAVE

When Biggie Smalls was murdered on March 9, 1997, he was gearing up to release his second album. That album's title? *Life After Death*. It came out just sixteen days later and topped the *Billboard* charts. Tracks that seemingly foreshadowed his end: "Somebody's Gotta Die," "Last Day," and "Miss U." The album cover even featured Biggie leaning up against a hearse, and the album's photography was shot in a graveyard in January 1997. "It's a powerful presence," photographer Michael Lavine told the *Undefeated* in 2017 about the symbolism in the cover. "It makes you feel like he works there, or presides over the souls. It's like his home."

YOU CAN SELL A CRAPLOAD OF MUSIC

After Lou Reed died in 2014, *Billboard* reported that his album sales jumped a whopping 607 percent the week after his passing; his band the Velvet Underground also saw a massive spike, selling 236 percent more albums than the previous week. That fact likely would have made Reed snarl. "If something of mine ever got popular . . . that was not the point," he told *Spin* in 2008. "I had other goals."

YOU CAN FINALLY RELEASE SOLO ALBUMS

In 2001, Ramones godfather Joey Ramone passed away at just forty-nine years old. A year later, his first-ever solo album, *Don't Worry About Me*, arrived, and in 2012, his second solo album, "*. . . Ya Know?*" came out.

YOU CAN PISS PEOPLE OFF

In 1994, fourteen years after his death, John Lennon "recorded" two new songs with the Beatles: "Real Love" and "Free as a Bird." Paul, Ringo, and George turned "lost" Lennon demos from the seventies into "new Beatles songs" that were included in the 1995 and 1996 compilation sets *Anthology 1* and *Anthology 2*. Critics hated it. Even random fans gave Macca a piece of their mind. "I had a rather obnoxious customs man when I was going through New York," McCartney told *Q* magazine in 1995. "He was very serious, a pasty lad, who said, 'The project you're doing with the Beatles . . .' Yeah? 'I just want to tell you that I don't consider it the Beatles without John.' I was in no mood after a plane flight, this guy's customs, I don't need this shit—I said, 'I don't care what you think, and it shows how much you know, cos John's fuckin on it!'"

WILCO

LAST SONG

"Turn! Turn! Turn!"

BY THE BYRDS (1965)

M Y FATHER PASSED AWAY A COUPLE of summers ago. We were all there with him, and one of the things we did a lot, as he was becoming less and less responsive, is we played music. So thinking about this made me think about that quite a bit.

One of the things we did play a lot of was "Night Train" by Earl Bostic. It's not a song that you would associate with morbidity. And that song worked its magic many times as he was getting sicker, almost to the point that he wanted to get up and dance. It was his go-to whenever he would talk about what his favorite song was. It had some sort of happy memory for him from when he was a young person.

That made me think that it's kinda nice to have some sort of full-circle connection to a song. And I think one of the first songs that I ever responded to that would feel sort of comforting in this scenario is "Turn! Turn! Turn!" by the Byrds. That's my choice. There's something pretty magical about this recording, not to mention that the lyrics are pretty appropriate and I think that's kind of what the song is about: there's a time for life and death. This is one of the first truly transformative pieces of music I encountered that changed my life in a way. It seems like a sweet thought to have one last listen.

I was born in '67, and I bet I was listening to that song by the time I was four or five. And I never really got sick of it. It was a remnant of my sister's and my aunt's teen years, because they're both about fifteen years older than I am. I just inherited their records when I was really, really young.

The structure of the song is pretty unique. It keeps folding in on itself somehow—and doesn't really have a verse/chorus structure. There's a forward momentum to the guitar part—and it's a unique sound that wasn't common to my ears at the time. For a lot of people, the Byrds' big calling card was the twelve-string guitar. It was kind of the Beatles' sound, but never really highlighted on Beatles recordings. It seems to be on those Byrds records. The whole song is pretty much sung in harmony, which is unusual. There's not really a singer on this song. There's a vocal that's a blend, for the most part, and that's kind of beautiful; it stops becoming a person and becomes a thing, singing these fairly emotional lyrics. But there's a detachment from them; I think it's one of the ways it succeeds in becoming more like scripture. If Pete Seeger's version is a guy reading the Bible, their version is more like a choir of angels explaining life and death or something.

The Byrds are pretty foundational, for sure, even for Uncle Tupelo. Without *Sweetheart of the Rodeo* and some of the transitions that they went through, we might not have found enough country to embrace, you know? To pursue it a little deeper. So that definitely led us down that path to Gram Parsons. Even like Merle Haggard and Merle Travis, and who they were covering. It's all a part of the stew, that time. But even beyond that—the early Byrds records basically taught me how to sing harmony and that's essentially what I did in Uncle Tupelo. So, I don't know how much you can value that as being a huge part of who I am or my musical career—but it's certainly where I learned it, singing along in the car with tapes of Byrds records. It's how I earned my keep.

When my father passed away, his girlfriend was playing a lot of Wilco, too. It was almost too much to contemplate at the time. It was almost too profound. I'd probably still cry about it if I thought about it too long. Everybody had made that decision before I had even gotten there. So it wasn't for me. It wasn't to make me feel good. But it was extremely touching. They were listening to the box set of outtakes and B sides. Some of those are things I hardly listen to, if ever. Apparently, my dad listened to them a lot. Which makes sense! As a contrarian, he would have thought most of those things should have been on the records and I had missed an opportunity with them.

My sons, Spencer and Sammy, and I did manage to play some songs for him when he was in the hospital and hospice, and at home, when we got to come back. You know, at the time, as sad as everything was, it did contribute to the overall feeling that what we were all experiencing was beautiful and natural and not entirely sad. Just a fact of life. Some relief, in him not being in pain or suffering anymore—but the idea that you can have a good death is not really something you think very often. To witness it, honestly, my predominant emotions were relief and gratitude; not loss and grief, oddly enough. I certainly felt loss

"Turn! Turn! Turn!"

ARTIST
The Byrds

ALBUM
Turn! Turn! Turn!

LENGTH
3 minutes, 49 seconds

REPORTED NUMBER OF TAKES IT TOOK TO GET THE FINAL VERSION
Seventy-eight!

NUMBER OF WEEKS AT NO. 1 ON THE BILLBOARD HOT 100
Three

ORIGINALLY WRITTEN BY
Pete Seeger, who cribbed most of the lyrics from the third chapter of the Book of Ecclesiastes. Only the phrase "Turn! Turn! Turn!" and the last line are new.

123

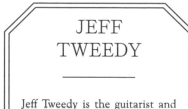

JEFF TWEEDY

Jeff Tweedy is the guitarist and vocalist of Wilco and the author of the *New York Times* bestselling memoir *Let's Go (So We Can Get Back)*.

and grief, but my predominant feeling was "God, that was a good way to go."

Everybody spends a lot of time being fearful when it comes to death. And death is like most anything you're fearful of because it's the unknown that you're trying to cope with. And it's the one thing aside from being born that we all have in common. Nobody who's been on the planet has not had that experience. I try to remind myself of that all the time.

Death is a pretty common theme in my lyrics. I think all writers have obsessions and I think a lot of writers have that very same obsession. There's a lot of good reasons for that. It constantly feels like it's something that you have to take the pulse of: How well am I doing today in coping with my mortality? It's a constant scab we're picking at. I personally think that it's important to do that. I would argue that, at the risk of it being a disabling obsession, I have continued to pursue those thoughts without moderating very much—I don't think it's a debilitating obsession. It's a way for me to remain clear, you know? I think a lot of people are motivated by their fear of death without being very conscious of it and it allows them to do some pretty negative things. But if you have it in the corner of your eye a lot of the time, for one thing, it allows you to be more appreciative on a day-to-day basis, more appreciative of your life. Being less compelled by your fear to shut down or tune out your fellow man.

YANNIS PHILIPPAKIS

FOALS

———

LAST SONG

"Tou Kitsos H Mana"

TRADITIONAL

M Y FATHER COMES FROM A VILLAGE in Greece on the island of Karpathos that has a very rich musical tradition. It's unique because it is an isolated village on a small, isolated island. So some of the songs they sing harken back to the Byzantine era—there are eleventh-century songs they sing. One of them is called "Tou Kitsos H Mana," which translates to "Kitso's Mother."

"Tou Kitsos H Mana"

WRITTEN BY
Unclear

WRITTEN IN
Unclear

LENGTH
Unclear

CAN YOU AT LEAST FIND IT ONLINE?
Good luck! There's a grainy YouTube of some guys singing it in a bar, I think. Which is pretty fitting for this song.

It's a beautiful song and a song that's been sung in the village for hundreds of years. It's passed down—that stuff isn't written down, there's no musical notation for it. And it's a song that makes me think about ancestry and death and the mountains. It's a transportive song for me, a soothing song. If I knew I was about to go, it would be a song that would make me think it's okay, because it's a song that connects me to all my ancestors.

I go back to this island fairly regularly now, but there was a period when I didn't go back. And although I'm surrounded by the music in general, that specific tune—I hadn't heard it for a while. I'd been touring and it was the longest stretch of time where I hadn't been back—about four years. My father picked me up at the airport, which is in the south of the island. It's about an hour and a half drive to get to the village. When you first see the village, it's a set of cubist houses that are perched on this mountainside. To get there, you have to go through super-windy, very dangerous roads. I was with my father and we were listening to a CD of his. We got closer and that song came on. The weather was gorgeous, the sun was about to set—it was one of those moments that is so distinct, it just stays with you.

I'm British and I love living in England. But I have no roots there. My mom is South African, my dad's Greek. I'm first-generation Brit and I don't have any extended family. When I go back to the village, we have a family coffee shop there. My great-grandfather had it, then my grandfather, and now my first cousin has it. That song would have been sung in that coffee shop. And it feels contained away from the rest of the world. That music that's played there—it's still of the place and not just part of the rest of the world. There's something about the isolation, the privacy, the preciousness, the rarity of it. They still sing it. I've sung this song with my friends, drunk, at two in the morning there. I can only do that there. There's something nice about that.

ONE LAST SONG

YANNIS PHILIPPAKIS

Yannis Philippakis is the lead singer and guitarist of British rock band Foals. Known for a killer live show, the band has performed all over the world and at major festivals, including Glastonbury, Primavera Sound, and Coachella.

My father sings and makes instruments that they play in the village. There was one recording of a musician from the village from Olympos—he died in the early nineties. He's not well known in Greece, but on the island, you just hear it. You just hear this music all the time. It's his version of that track. Ioannis Pavlidis. He's like the OG. He passed away thirty years ago and he's still the guy—he set the benchmark. His voice is stunning. He had a huge knowledge of the material. He lived it.

When I hear this song, it sets me in that landscape. And it sets me above a cliff, so it has the sea, it has the mountains, it has the wind. I think it's a song where it would just be right for the last one to hear.

If I extract just the music away from the landscape and all of the meaning attached to it—there's scent attached to it for me, and there's time. When you're driving up, it smells good. All of that is linked into the song. It connects you to these prior ages—I don't think there are that many scenarios where you have a piece of living tradition that connects you back five hundred years.

ONE LAST SONG

BETTYE LAVETTE

LAST SONG

"Clair de Lune"

BY CLAUDE DEBUSSY (1890 OR 1905)

I GREW UP IN A HOUSE WHERE THERE WAS a jukebox in the living room instead of a couch. I had a teenage sister and I had a father who liked gospel and blues and a mother who liked popular tunes and country and western. So I grew up listening to everything, and I knew as many songs by Red Foley as I did by B. B. King and the Five and Dime Boys. At the tender age of just eighteen months, I learned all these songs on the jukebox. I didn't know songs from different genres. I just thought they were all songs. I didn't know they were country songs or blues songs.

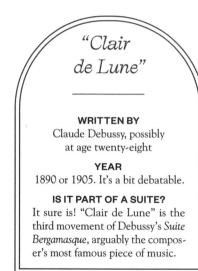

BETTYE LAVETTE

Bettye Lavette's first recording was made in 1962, when she was sixteen. She's done it all throughout her lengthy career: found success as a disco artist, acted onstage, and performed at President Obama's inauguration. In 2020, she was inducted into the Blues Hall of Fame.

"Clair de Lune"

WRITTEN BY
Claude Debussy, possibly at age twenty-eight

YEAR
1890 or 1905. It's a bit debatable.

IS IT PART OF A SUITE?
It sure is! "Clair de Lune" is the third movement of Debussy's *Suite Bergamasque*, arguably the composer's most famous piece of music.

If you were black and you wanted a drink after work in 1946 in western Michigan, you had to come to my house. You couldn't go anywhere else; my mother sold corn liquor right out of our house. You could buy pints and shots, chicken sandwiches, fish sandwiches, barbecue sandwiches. And nobody could cuss but my mother. This wasn't a place to cheat on someone; nobody could come without their true partner—you couldn't meet your girlfriend there. If anybody got hit, it was likely my mother doing the hitting.

So, I've always felt that I was a part of the music. I've never quite looked at it as if I was a fan. I've never had moments where I was like, "This is my favorite tune."

But Debussy's "Clair de Lune" is the most beautiful song I've ever heard in my life. I've never heard another melody that peaceful and relaxing. It sounds as if it's not supposed to be a part of music; it's a nether song. I think there's a haunting quality to it, a sadness to it, a longing in it. The longing of not even knowing what you're longing for. You can just recognize this longing whether you're longing for anything or not. That's the way it sounds to me, like being out on the ocean and looking at nothing but water.

I'm always attracted to melody, which is why it's so hard for me to like a song that doesn't have a good melody, no matter how strong the words are. Melody is what soothes me. That's what appeals. Often, I'll find I fall in love with the melody but then the words are no good. "Clair de Lune" doesn't put you through those fixes: you just have this beautiful melody and that's it.

When I first went on the road with a Broadway musical, my manager looped "Clair de Lune" for me on a recording and I could listen to it over and over until I fell asleep. It's the only thing I can fall asleep to. I won't deliberately listen to anything else. This I can just drift off to. I've been listening to it for at least fifty years.

131

THE GENIUS
GUIDE TO
SONGS
ABOUT
DEATH

WHAT ARE THE MOST MORBID SONGS OUT there? That's not an easy question to answer. But Genius.com, the online database where you go to look up the lyrics of that Drake song you just can't quite remember, has a window into this question.

I asked them how many songs have the word *death*, *devil*, *murder*, *dying*, or *died* in the lyrics. They essentially told me those words are so common in music, if they ran an analysis, their machines might explode.

Okay, fine. I had to get creative. Instead, they ran several analyses looking into different euphemisms for dying. Here's what they found when exploring more than three million songs by three hundred thousand different artists.

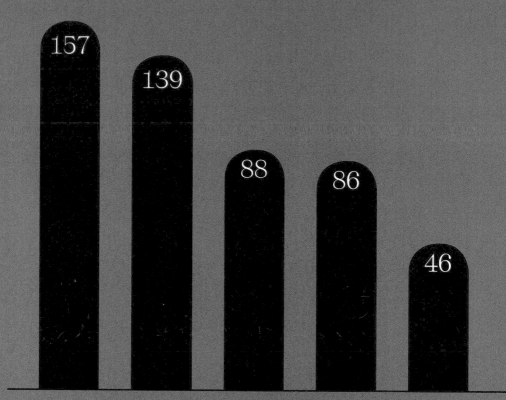

157	139	88	86	46
"SIX FEET UNDER"	"DEARLY DEPARTED"	"MEET YOUR MAKER"	"CROAK"	"KICK THE BUCKET"
I mean, you're pretty dead at this point, and using this really drives home the point that you or someone is/should be/ is going to be buried soon.	Using this is almost a grand gesture, like you're addressing a crowd of people at a funeral but really talking to the deceased at his/her funeral. Honestly, this is kind of weird to do. But in a lyric—it's fine. You can address your missed loved ones, and it's not that weird.	Use this in a song and you're most likely threatening someone. Like, "Keep grabbing fries from my lunch tray and you're gonna meet your maker."	Honestly, this is a pretty funny slang term for dying—it's the language of frogs! So if you hear this in a lyric, you gotta take it with a grain of salt. I can't imagine a line about dying using the word "croak" and choking anyone up.	In my Genius research, I learned that the most rhymed phrase with this saying is "fuck it." So, if you're going to use this in a song, really think twice about rhyming it with "fuck it." It's played out!

GENIUS GUIDE TO SONGS ABOUT DEATH

In this chart, you'll see how often different slang death sayings showed up in Genius's database. Below is a very unscientific, not-data-driven-at-all, analysis of what these stats really mean.

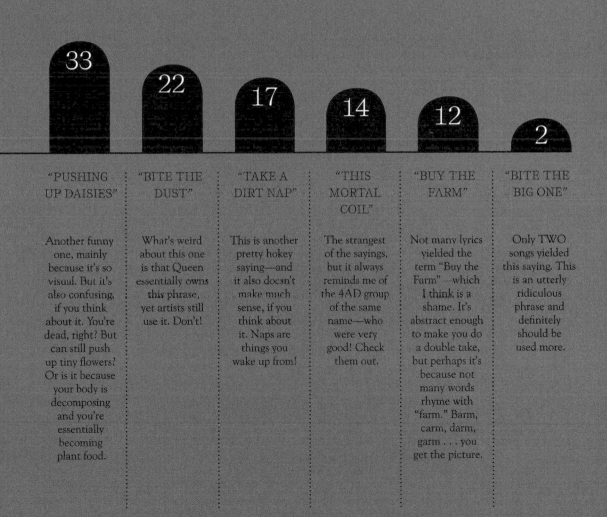

33	22	17	14	12	2
"PUSHING UP DAISIES"	"BITE THE DUST"	"TAKE A DIRT NAP"	"THIS MORTAL COIL"	"BUY THE FARM"	"BITE THE BIG ONE"
Another funny one, mainly because it's so visual. But it's also confusing, if you think about it. You're dead, right? But can still push up tiny flowers? Or is it because your body is decomposing and you're essentially becoming plant food.	What's weird about this one is that Queen essentially owns this phrase, yet artists still use it. Don't!	This is another pretty hokey saying—and it also doesn't make much sense, if you think about it. Naps are things you wake up from!	The strangest of the sayings, but it always reminds me of the 4AD group of the same name—who were very good! Check them out.	Not many lyrics yielded the term "Buy the Farm"—which I think is a shame. It's abstract enough to make you do a double take, but perhaps it's because not many words rhyme with "farm." Barm, carm, darm, garm . . . you get the picture.	Only TWO songs yielded this saying. This is an utterly ridiculous phrase and definitely should be used more.

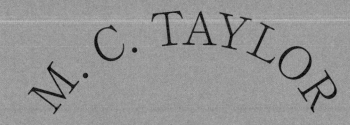

M. C. TAYLOR

HISS GOLDEN MESSENGER

LAST SONG

"*Anymore for Anymore*"

BY RONNIE LANE (1974)

D O YOU KNOW THE AUTHOR GEORGE Saunders? He's one of the greats. He said something like "Things get really interesting when death comes into the room." I've always thought about that and it's absolutely true. Whatever your relationship with death— however it touched your life—just to meditate on the idea, that it's going to happen to you, and everybody you love, makes things interesting. And more heightened. And some people don't want to live in that heightened state all the time. Including me. I feel like part of the vulnerability in my songs is that engagement with death.

Ronnie Lane and "Anymore for Anymore"

MEMBER OF
The Small Faces and then the Faces

1974
The year the album *Anymore for Anymore* was released, after he quit the Faces because Rod Stewart was being lame.

RECORDED AT
Ronnie Lane's Mobile Studio, one of the first mobile recording studios—it was an Airstream trailer. Other remarkable albums that used this: the Who's *Quadrophenia* and Led Zeppelin's *Physical Graffiti*.

LENGTH
3 minutes, 43 seconds

IS THE SONG "ANYMORE FOR ANYMORE" ABOUT DEATH?
Perhaps! I mean, these lines are pretty death-y: "Anymore for anymore / Hear those angels say / But anymore's too much for me / I'm goin' on my way."

M. C. TAYLOR

M. C. Taylor writes and records music as Hiss Golden Messenger. Since starting the project in 2006, he's released numerous albums, including six on legendary North Carolina indie label Merge Records.

When I first started digging into Ronnie Lane's *Anymore for Anymore*, I had just moved to North Carolina and my wife and I were living out in the country, from Chapel Hill. And it was the springtime, very green. The man who owned the land we were living on was out mowing. I remember sitting in my office and looking out over the fields and listening to that record and the smell of cut grass was so strong. There was something at that moment that connected me to that record.

I like that he's addressing someone in the title track. He's about to accompany someone on a journey. I like that. That's a nice welcome. That recording was made outside. If you listen closely, you can hear the wind on the microphones, you can hear his kids—or a kid that was around—in the background. I just think that's beautiful. That makes a song that's already powerful more so to me. It's casual. I don't know if they intended to use that recording or what—but the vibe is just so strong. It's life. They put up some microphones and there they are. It's a perfect recording to me.

At the same time, I don't think what Ronnie Lane does with his music is any reinvention. But he combines a lot of American traditions, which at the time Americans weren't quite doing. It took an outsider to pick and choose his favorite parts of country, blues, gospel, vaudeville, and make it one thing. You don't hear a lot of that in his contemporaries that were American. And the other thing, he was just a . . . I don't mean to name this a pejorative term, but he was on the losing end of life. Once he quit the Faces, his life wasn't particularly easy. He didn't have a whole lot of success. Maybe that's where I recognize myself in his journey: he kept doing it because he loved it and he was good at it.

SAM BEAM

IRON & WINE

LAST SONG

"*É De Manhã*"

BY CAETANO VELOSO (1963)

S ONGS ARE SO FUNNY. THERE ARE NO rules with songs. That's what's so fun about them. I find what I like about a song, there's no logic to it. And that's what I love. You're reacting to these vibrations and it's all this emotional attachment—and a lot of the time, it makes no sense. It depends on how old you are, what you're bringing to it, as much as what the song is actually doing.

SAM BEAM

Iron & Wine has been the principal songwriting vehicle for Sam Beam for nearly twenty years. His music has been used in numerous films and TV shows; he frequently records with other artists, too, and has released collaborative albums with Calexico, Jesca Hoop, and Ben Bridwell of Band of Horses.

"É De Manhã"

ARTIST
Caetano Veloso

GENRE
Tropicalia

TRANSLATES TO
"It's Morning"

WRITTEN IN
1963

LENGTH
Unknown . . . but not terribly long

FIRST APPEARS ON
Velosa's sister Maria Bethânia's 1965 self-titled album

Right now I'm obsessed with a Caetano Veloso song. He's a Brazilian artist and this song, "É de Manhã," I hear it and it makes me want to weep. And I have no idea what he's saying. It's probably a song about a bird.

So, right now, my contribution to this, is a song I have no idea what it's about. It's just the tonality of his voice that makes me want to weep. It's the most beautiful piece of music ever. There's equal parts beauty and dissonance. It's fragile.

I mean, there's so many different songs. They're all colors on the palette. And I don't ruminate on death. I'm not a morbid person. But when I sit down to write a song, for some reason, it seems like a time to say something that I mean instead of making a joke. It's kind of like if I step into a church, I'm supposed to say something I mean.

So that's it. Caetano Veloso's "É de Manhã." I'm telling you: openly weep. It's wonderful. You're going to listen and go, "Pfft," but I think it's the most beautiful thing I've heard in a long time. Since you're asking me today what I want to hear, this is it.

REGINA SPEKTOR

LAST SONG

"Requiem"

BY MOZART (1791)

I TEND TO HAVE MUCH MORE OF AN eastern European Jewish superstitious nature, like *tuh*, *tuh*, *tuh*, don't talk about shit that's scary or bad. So at first, I was like, "I don't want to talk about this." But I was also thinking—I don't know if that's the job of songs. Because I was thinking about the job of music. What it does for us. I think the reason there's so much music in the world is that it means so many different things to people—and because it has so many different jobs for people. Have you ever met people who say they don't listen to the lyrics?

REGINA SPEKTOR

Regina Spektor was born in Moscow and moved to the Bronx, New York, at age nine. She has released seven albums over the course of her near-twenty-year career, and her music has been used numerous times in television and film, including as the title song for Netflix's acclaimed series *Orange Is the New Black*.

That's always been a surprising thing for me. They just say, "Yeah, I don't really listen to the words. I just listen to the song." Or they'll say, "It's just about the beat"—where they feel it. For somebody, it's what will push them to run a marathon. Or for somebody else, it will allow for them to have a good cry. For somebody else, it allows them to have experiences or perspectives outside themselves. It's all so different for people.

And if you think of the moment of dying, as much as you can conceive of it, from my experience of it, it doesn't seem like a moment of song. So I was trying to think about it for a while, and I was like, I don't know if I really have a good answer. The only thing that kept coming back to me—and it might sound morbid, because it has to do with death—is Mozart's Requiem. I discovered it when I was fifteen, when my parents gave it to me as a birthday present or a New Year's present. I never really had a lot of CDs, because we didn't buy CDs. We were tight on cash, and that's just not where money went. But they bought me this CD of Mozart's Requiem conducted by Herbert Von Karajan. It's one of my favorite pieces of music. I used to listen to it every night that year. It was one of those things that made perfect sense. It was elevating. Everything got elevated to a higher level.

I had this CD and I had it forever. But I'm not very good at taking care of my things, which is one of my many problems in the world. I got it really scratched up after years and years of not being handled gently. And then I couldn't find it for forever—that recording. I didn't love anything else. And I kept looking. I would listen to another recording, and they would pronounce something slightly different or have a different tambour or a slightly different tempo. And it drove me crazy. It's like a key that couldn't fit a lock. And then years and years later, I remember talking to somebody about that. They were like, "Just look it up again. There's so much stuff on Spotify."

144

Now that I've rediscovered it, I've been listening to it for years. It's just very, very important to me. I think it's something about Mozart. There are just so many songs that are Russian, rock, folk, that I love and move me. A key to a special place. The Beatles, Bob Dylan, certain voices. But something about Mozart and the fact that he was very young when he died. This was the last piece he wrote, and it wasn't finished before he died. It got finished by one of his students. So it's something written so close to the edge. Nobody really gets to go there and come back, but people get really close to the edge. His music language is already so holy—that, combined with the structure of a requiem, when you listen to it, it bypasses certain things in your intellect and speaks directly to parts of your soul.

Requiem

WRITTEN IN
1791

LENGTH OF VON KARAJAN'S 1986 PERFORMANCE
52 minutes

WHY WAS MOZART WRITING THIS? WAS HE SCORING HIS OWN DEATH?
Hardly. He was actually commissioned to write Requiem for count Franz von Walsegg, who wanted this to be performed at the anniversary of the passing of his wife. Von Walsegg was kinda a jerk, known for buying musical compositions and passing them off as his own! And he was going to do this with the Requiem, too. But Mozart unexpectedly died during its composition, and his wife, Constance, had it finished in a hush-hush manner—so that it could still be delivered and she could get the final payment owed.

145

SONGS
FAMOUS TV
CHARACTERS
WENT
OUT TO

W ANNA HEAR SOMETHING WEIRD? I BET you can picture exactly where you were and who you were with when your favorite TV character died. But it makes sense! It's often a shocking and brutal assault on our psyche that leaves us emotionally drained for days, if not for weeks or months.

Unlike movie characters, where we are with them for maybe two hours, we are spending hours upon hours living with the storylines of TV characters. Their highs and lows as human beings, the things about life that make them struggle and overcome. More than any other art form, TV in the last twenty years has connected us to characters deeply—which makes choosing the music they die to a monumental task.

Here's a look at nine different ways music is used to soundtrack deaths from some of the biggest shows of this century. Spoilers ahead, obviously.

147

THE SONG THAT ENCAPSULATES THE JOURNEY
BREAKING BAD

In the final scene of *Breaking Bad*, the anti-hero of all antiheroes, Walter White, gets shot in a meth lab—a fitting end to his journey from high school chemistry teacher with cancer to southwest drug kingpin. The final song, Badfinger's "Baby Blue," was chosen by creator Vince Gilligan.

"Walter's death is essentially introduced in the pilot episode. He's given a death sentence," says *Breaking Bad*'s music supervisor, Thomas Golubić. "It led me down many different avenues—and a lot were pretentious or not true to the character. The Badfinger song was picked by Vince. It was on an early mixtape we had—we put together a list of songs that had a 'Blue' theme to them. But it was one of those things we never expected to use. We tended to not be very on the nose about music on that show. It's a love song. It has a real sweet, wistful quality. He's not exiting in a bad or tragic way. It would have been dishonest of us to choose a critical song. We didn't want to leave with the audience judging the character. Having it end on a love song was appropriate for everybody."

THE SONG THAT SAYS NOTHING AT ALL—OR DOES IT?
THE WIRE

In some instances, songs are just part of the scenery and have nothing to do with the actual character's death. In the case of *The Wire*'s Omar, he was in a Korean bodega buying cigarettes. And what would be playing in a Korean deli? Korean music, of course. In this case, music supervisor Blake Leyh found a song that was performing well at the time on the Korean pop charts—"Let This as Nothing Happened" by Choi Suk Jun.

"This choice is a great example of [creator] David [Simon]'s aesthetic. The way Omar dies is completely random. So the music is exactly the same," says Leyh. "In *The Wire* we were not trying to heighten the emotions or tell the viewer what to think. We were just trying to make the environment more realistic and more authentic. It's a Korean deli. So what music do they play in a Korean deli? Rather than get some library music that sounds like Korean music—I actually went and looked at Korean pop music that was known, that was a hit."

THE SONG THAT TELLS THE SCENE WHAT TO DO

THE SOPRANOS

Did Tony die in the final scene of *The Sopranos*? It's a notion that will likely be debated until the end of time, and creator David Chase has been coy about it in the years that followed the finale. Let's go ahead and say he was whacked in front of his family in that diner—the last song was Journey's "Don't Stop Believin'," a tune that somehow screams "Jersey" and "Tony" all at once. There's hope but also a darkness that resides in the lyrics, and that was Tony in pretty much every episode.

Chase has been asked about that final scene ad nauseam over the years, but in 2015, he broke down the song choice extensively for the Directors Guild of America. "It's almost like the soundtrack of his life, because he sees various songs," Chase said of Tony flipping through the jukebox. "No matter what song we picked, I wanted it to be a song that would have been from Tony's high school years, or his youth. That's what he would have played. When I wrote it, there were three songs in contention for this last song, and 'Don't Stop Believin'' was the one that seemed to work the best. I think it's a really good rock 'n' roll song. The music is very important to me in terms of the timing of the scene, the rhythm of the scene. The song dictates part of the pace. And having certain lyrics of the song, and certain instrumental flourishes happen in certain places, dictates what the cuts will be. I directed the scene to fit the song. The singing gets more and more strident and more invested as the song goes along. Musically it starts to build and build into something as it's just about to release. And when you look at the scene, you get that feeling."

THE SONG THAT'S TIED TO STORYLINES
GAME OF THRONES

Game of Thrones deaths were so in vogue by the time the final season rolled around, friends, offices, families—everyone—were making bets on who would die. The series made death desirable: you wanted some characters to die because they were insufferable and deserved it. But it was a massacre from mid-way through the series, the Red Wedding scene where Robb Stark and crew are ambushed, that utilized music in a way that tied together characters, storyline, and sound. As the scene starts to unfold, musicians at the ceremony start to subtly play the song "The Rains of Castamere," which was essentially the theme song of House Lannister. And everyone in Westeros knew this—including Lady Stark, who realized it and started to panic, and rightfully so. Moments later, her throat is slit, her son is murdered, too, and blood is everywhere.

Ramin Djawadi, who wrote the series music, began working on this piece of music years before we'd all see that fateful wedding. Djawadi's task was to create something viewers would always recognize as some Lannister shit. It shows up a few times in odd spots before the big event—for example, Tyrion Lannister can be heard whistling the melody in season two. "By the time we get to season three, it's a known theme that viewers will identify with the Lannisters—so when you hear it, you will know something is off, and that this melody does not belong at this wedding," Djawadi told the *Hollywood Reporter* in 2019.

A SONG FOR DEATH
LOST

In *Lost*, characters were marooned on a mysterious island that had tons of insanity going on around every corner. The showrunners used pop music at times throughout the six seasons, but for most of the music you heard, the score was composed by Oscar-winning composer Michael Giacchino.

At the end of the third season, the rock and roll bassist Charlie Pace drowned in one of the series's more memorable scenes—he dies in an underwater station control room (of course), and viewers watch as the little room he's in fills up with water. The music playing is a composition called "Life and Death," written by Giacchino, and was used whenever a character left the island by dying.

"Sometimes you can be very manipulative with music, but in the case of *Lost* generally, I'm just giving you how I feel about it," Giacchino told the *Los Angeles Times* in 2010 as the show was concluding. "It's because I like the show so much. So for me, it's about transferring my reaction to the show. If you are sitting there crying, that means I was sad too."

A SONG THAT EVERYONE ASSOCIATES WITH DEATH— BUT HAS TO REMAIN TRUE TO THE SHOW

THE O.C.

The teen drama *The O.C.* was special in many ways, like filling a void that *Beverly Hills, 90210* left when it went off the air in 2000 and introducing the world at large to Peter Gallagher's amazing eyebrows. But the show also did something revolutionary: the writers killed off Marissa Cooper, arguably the main character next to Ryan Atwood, in the third season. (Okay, ratings were going down, and the fourth season would end up being its last. But still.) The show had been using prominent indie artists with the guidance of music supervisor Alexandra Patsavas, and for Marissa's moment, where Ryan pulls her out of a car crash and carries her down the street in a gloriously shot dark scene, they asked singer-songwriter Imogen Heap to cover Leonard Cohen's masterpiece "Hallelujah"—a song that at the time wasn't oversaturated.

"I remember conversations about how we could make this heartbreaking, but still in our template," Patsavas recalls. "It has to feel like the show—or otherwise it takes you out. In this case, we didn't try a lot of things. We determined before the scene was shot that Imogen should do it."

A SONG THAT TIED EVERYTHING TOGETHER

SIX FEET UNDER

Death was the plot point in HBO's *Six Feet Under*, which followed the Fisher family as they navigated life as the owners of a funeral home. So it would only be fitting that the series's creator, Alan Ball, chose to wrap up the show with a death montage that shows the fate of all the characters sometime in the future. The song playing over the scene is Sia's "Breathe Me"—at the time, Sia was best known as a vocalist for the British electronic duo Zero 7. It would be years before she found mainstream success in the United States.

"The power of Sia's 'Breathe Me' stitched it all together," says Thomas Golubić, who also worked on this show. "It had such an emotional impact and was so unique at the time. It carried that whole sequence to a close and I think was ultimately very satisfying. Each character had a different kind of death—which was extremely challenging. A lot of us feared the ending wasn't going to work. And we had a four-minute-and-twenty-second song that was supposed to fit into a six-minute-and-forty-second sequence. That meant we had to extend the song. That was a miracle in editing."

151

A SONG THAT'S LYRICALLY ON POINT
MAD MEN

Aside from the death of the sixties, when *Mad Men* went off the air, most of the characters had survived. But not everyone. Toward the end of season five, Lane Pryce, the British executive at Sterling Cooper, hung himself in his office, a suicide driven by his embezzlement scandal.

Nothing played during this scene—that wasn't creator Matt Weiner's style. But as the show cut to the credits moments later, the Lovin' Spoonful's "Butchie's Tune" came on, where the opening lyrics say:

> *Don't give me a place for my*
> *memories to stay*
> *Don't show me an inn or a light*
> *to find the way*
> *I ain't got time for the things on*
> *your mind*
> *And I'm leavin' you today*
> *On my way*

"The lyrical tie-in was so critical and on point," says Alexandra Patsavas, who worked on this show, too. "So many of the songs were scripted—but some were not. I felt like it was my job to make sure we got it. These are classic tracks and some of them had clearance issues, where it was difficult finding the people that could approve. We needed to make sure, too, that the music was as accurate as the rest of the show."

A SONG THAT TIES THE SERIES TOGETHER
GREY'S ANATOMY

Sometimes a song becomes anthemic to a series. In *Grey's Anatomy*, Shonda Rhimes and Alexandra Patsavas found this with Snow Patrol's "Chasing Cars" and used it to soundtrack two major death scenes: first, Denny Duquette in season two, and then Derek Shepherd, aka McDreamy, in season eleven.

But for McDreamy's death, instead of using the exact same version, Patsavas got hold of a cover version by Chicago-based songwriter Ryan O'Neal, who performs under the moniker Sleeping at Last. That way, the musical thread continues but is different.

And there was drama.

"Shonda intended for this cover to go into the next episode," Patsavas says. "I sent her this very early in the morning, when the show with Derek's death scene was supposed to air. There was another song in that moment, and Shonda loved the [Sleeping at Last] version so much—we scrambled like I've never scrambled so much before, to clear the song and ready it for air that same day. She was like, "I love the song, it makes me cry, and it has to be here." It was emotional, but a new version—but important to the show and audience. If the lyrics are right—there are always ways of making things poignant."

LAST SONG

"*Amazing Grace*"

BY JOHN NEWTON (1779)

W HEN I WAS YOUNGER I WOULD GO
to church on occasion—I thought that was all
there was to the idea of faith. But sometime after
that, the Lord just sank deep in my heart and said, "You've
never walked with me. You believe in God. Believe also in
me." He is the way to God. He was God to human form. He
paid the debt for our sins. I think "Amazing Grace" pretty well
says it all. A gift as wonderful as salvation, and knowing that
when you die, you will spend eternity with God in heaven—
that isn't just automatic. We do have to receive it.

WANDA JACKSON

Known as "the Queen of Rockabilly," Wanda Jackson has been in the music business since the 1950s. In her early days, she often performed with Elvis Presley, and she has released more than thirty albums. In recent years, she's collaborated with modern musicians: In 2009, she teamed up with Jack White on her album *The Party Ain't Over*, and in 2012, Justin Townes Earle produced her album *Unfinished Business*. In 2005, she was awarded a National Heritage Fellowship, a lifetime achievement award from the National Endowment for the Arts.

I know that I would want to leave hearing something that has some meaning. I wouldn't want to just hear "Honky Tonk Angels" or something. I'd like it to be something more indicative of my life and what I'd like to say. And that's probably "Amazing Grace." People who don't know Jesus Christ personally, they could hear something like that—that salvation is a free gift from God. It's for all of us. We don't have to work our way to heaven; we just have to receive what Christ has already done for us. He paid the ultimate price—paid for our sins. But we do have to receive it. If I give you a gift, it really isn't yours until you reach out and take it. And so that's the way it is with God and salvation. You accept his free forgiveness and salvation.

I had a ministry for about eighteen years. And then God began to open the doors in the secular field once again. God was saying, "Now you're strong in Christ. Now I want you to go into the world and tell the world what I did with your life." And that's what I've been doing—telling people Christ has come into my life and made a wonderful difference. I don't belabor all that I do. I know that something wonderful happened to me and it can happen to them, too. I have a lot of gospel out there. It's not current right now, because I've been recording secular music. But every one of my albums has a gospel in it. I feel like that's what the Lord wants of me right now—to sing rockabilly songs, make people happy, bring back memories for them.

If you truly listen to "Amazing Grace," if you know Christ, it's a happy song. Wonderful. If you haven't received Christ in your life, it's sure to bring conviction. You do need God in your life to be fulfilled. I think that song says it very well. I also like "Lord, I'm Coming Home," which is a beautiful song about having strayed from God and now turning back to him. And I used that when we had our ministry. I threw a Gospel concert and gave my testimony. We would do altar calls to anyone. After the congregation had heard

155

"Amazing Grace"

ARTIST
John Newton, a British
born-again Christian.

FIRST PUBLISHED
1779

**HOW MANY VERSIONS
ARE OUT THERE?**
A ton. According to the Library
of Congress, they have more than
three thousand known versions of
the song by different musicians.

**A FEW VERSIONS BY
FAMOUS MUSICIANS (AND
ONE PRESIDENT) WORTH
TRACKING DOWN**
Elvis Presley, Johnny Cash, the
Dropkick Murphys, LeAnn Rimes,
Janis Joplin, Phish, Alan Jackson,
Sufjan Stevens, Chet Atkins, the
Byrds, Willie Nelson, and President
Obama.

our story, we would ask if anyone wanted to give their life to Christ. So we saw many people come to the Lord and many people who turned back to him.

I think about death a lot. At this age you think more about it than when you're in your thirties, forties, fifties, and sixties. But I feel like, as a Christian—it's not that we're afraid of dying. We all have that fear. What's it going to be like? Don't you have that? You wonder. I'm not anxious to die. But I am not afraid of death. I know I have a place waiting for me and Christ will be there to walk with me. I'm at peace with all of that. So God has everything in place for me. Pretty wonderful, huh?

ROSANNE CASH

"Gold and Glass"

BY JAKOB LEVENTHAL (2019)

I THOUGHT OF THIS STORY I HEARD ABOUT Ronald Reagan. I wasn't a fan of Ronald Reagan, but this story deeply moved me. When he was in the depths of Alzheimer's, toward the end of his life, it was his birthday. They rolled in this big birthday cake, in the shape of the White House. And Nancy said to him, "Do you know what that is?" and he said, "No. But I think it has something to do with me."

"Gold and Glass"

ARTIST
Jakob Leventhal

ALBUM
Oh, So Bittersweet!

LENGTH
3 minutes, 6 seconds

IS THIS SONG ABOUT DEATH?
No, but it's not exactly a happy-go-lucky tune either.

"I wrote the song in like fifteen minutes; it just sort of came out, and it went through zero changes before we recorded it," Leventhal says. "It's about a lot of stuff—mostly emotionally about feeling like nothing you ever do and nothing anyone else does for you will make you happy, and then just sort of feeling despondent about that. Not an uplifter."

And that story moved me so much. He had lost everything; he had had this enormous life, been the leader of the free world, and lived in the most iconic structure in America. He had changed the course of history. But he sees this cake and says, "I think it has something to do with me." It represents this enormous life in back of him that has just trickled down to this tiny moment.

So, I was thinking the last song I'd want to hear, I'd want it to be that birthday cake in the shape of the White House. I would want it to be a song that said to me, "This had something to do with you."

Would it be a song I had written on my own? Would it be a song I wrote with my husband? Would it be one of my dad's songs? To say: *This is your life.* You weren't just an observer, and audience member. *This has something to do with you.*

I thought that it had to be a song by my son, Jakob. That is context and content and macro and micro all rolled into one. It has something to do with me, and it has something to do with any part of my legacy that will live on, any part of my DNA that will live on, so it stretches past and future.

It would provide a lot of comfort if I was leaving, that my musical lineage, back all the way to melancholy Scottish ballads, is going into the future with my son. And he's a great songwriter. He's distilled three, four, five generations of songwriting. It's shocking.

He made his first album a few years ago and is just finishing his second. And I thought it almost doesn't matter which song of his—it's the fact that it's the birthday cake.

But there's this song he wrote called "Gold and Glass," and there are these lines in it that say, "It's oh so bittersweet, it's such a treat . . . to be loved by anyone at all." That sorta sums it up. The most important thing was who you loved, how you loved, and who loved you back.

158

ROSANNE CASH

Rosanne Cash is a singer-songwriter, author, and member of the Nashville Songwriters Hall of Fame. Her latest album is 2018's *She Remembers Everything*. Music runs her in family: her father was country legend Johnny Cash.

The first time I heard it I was sitting there, weeping. Jake's a deep soul. He wrote these songs when he was seventeen, eighteen years old. It provides some comfort to me. I feel a responsibility for my musical legacy and carrying it on—and I hear what he's done and I'm like, *We're all safe.*

He synthesizes from stuff before his time, like the Beach Boys or the Beatles, along with singer-songwriters he's been influenced by, like Elliott Smith and Conor Oberst. And he brings a very dark twist to it.

I've thought about the melodies I've sung for forty years and some of my oldest songs—those have worn neural pathways into me. I saw that with my dad, too. There were rhythms that repeated even in the way he walked and moved. Melodies—I do think they embed themselves in us. If you're a musician and you've played a song four thousand times, it's definitely in your bloodstream.

PHOEBE BRIDGERS

LAST SONG

"Heavy Water/ I'd Rather Be Sleeping"

BY GROUPER (2008)

I THOUGHT OF THIS THE WAY I DO WHEN someone asks me what my favorite band is. I just answer for the moment. I can't relate it to other times in my life; I just have to answer for right now. Like, if I were to die tomorrow, what would be the song I pick? I have playlists and playlists of music I'd love to listen to in my final hours. But I don't know—Grouper's "Heavy Water/I'd Rather Be Sleeping" just struck me as ambiguous enough, and emotional enough—and I'm never sad when it comes on.

"Heavy Water/I'd Rather Be Sleeping"

ALBUM
Dragging a Dead Deer up a Hill

LENGTH
2 minutes, 53 seconds

WHAT IS IT ABOUT, IF ANYTHING?
Dreams. And Love. And water. Probably.

BUT IS IT ON IMPORTANT LISTS?
Yes! It's #67 on NPR's 200 Greatest Songs by 21st Century Women; *Dragging a Dead Deer Up a Hill* is #6 on Pitchfork's The 30 Best Dream Pop Albums.

PHOEBE BRIDGERS

Phoebe Bridgers is an acclaimed singer-songwriter based out of Los Angeles. She's also one-half of Better Oblivion Community Center with Conor Oberst and one-third of boygenius, alongside Lucy Dacus and Julien Baker. Her latest album is *Punisher*, released in 2020.

I would love something that would leave enough room for what's going on in my head. I don't want to be forced into some type of mood. I want something to inform whatever mood I'm having. I've listened to this song tripping on MDMA with somebody. And I've also listened to this song when I'm writing an essay or just lying in a field, in Silverlake, looking up at the sky. It gives you room. What I love about Grouper is, it's classical music for people who listen to indie rock. It's instrumental music, but it has words—a poem that is so beautiful. Why did she write the lyrics? She technically didn't have to.

I first heard this when I was in the middle of recording my first album, and I hung out with this friend of mine, Jeremy, who used to play in my high school band. He was like, you need to check out Grouper, you're going to love it. He played it for me in the car; it's hard for me to listen to music in that environment, but this was immediately effective and made me feel like I was practicing witchcraft or something.

Weirdly, I have a different relationship to death than other people who write music. I'm not obsessed with how I'm going to die, when I'm going to die, if there's an afterlife. It's crazy that it happens to everybody, and it's crazy that it's an equalizer. But I'm pretty separated from it. Maybe that's just dissociating, but I just can't think about it. Death is not my intrusive thought.

163

LUCINDA WILLIAMS

LAST SONG

"Shenandoah"

TRADITIONAL

I CAN REMEMBER IT WAS ONE DAY, PROBABLY when I was seventeen, and I suddenly realized, "Oh, nobody can protect me." It was the day I realized my vulnerability and my mortality. Before that, there's that time in your life as a child, and maybe as a teenager, where you don't think about the whole idea of dying. But once you have this realization, life just changes after that.

I've heard that when people are on their deathbeds, friends or family members will make a tape of songs for that person. One of my songs, "Lake Charles," has a line in it about a guy I knew, Clyde, who died. He had been sent back home to die, after being in the hospital. My friend Margaret Moser, who was the music writer for the *Austin Chronicle* for many, many years—she and Clyde were real close. And she made him a tape of Delta blues songs and R&B songs and took it to him and played it for him. She was with him at the moment of death and described it—a tear came from his eye. That's where I got the idea for the line "Did an angel whisper in those long last moments." I've always been fascinated by that. How that feels. The last moment. I bring it up in a song I wrote for the musician Vic Chesnutt, who took his own life. In "Seeing Black," I sing, "When did you start seeing black? When did you start seeing red? When did you start seeing white?" which I imagined to be the last stage. "Tell me, baby, what it's like."

I do refer to death quite a bit in my songs. It's been such an experience as I've gotten older. There've been so many losses.

I've just lost another friend to suicide. Gary Stewart. He worked at Rhino Records back in the eighties when I moved to LA. I was performing in Minneapolis after hearing of his death and performed that song "Seeing Black." I talked to people during that show about suicide a little bit. I said, "We don't need to be spending money on walls, we need to be spending more money on mental health care," and making sure people get the medications they need, the proper antidepressants. Because I take them.

The major song I wrote about suicide was "Sweet Old World." I had people tell me they were thinking about suicide and they heard that song somewhere and it changed their minds. Or, people would use it at a memorial service, when they lost someone to suicide. This whole suicide thing has been something that's grabbed me and made me wonder.

For my last song, I guess it would be a song that would make me cry every time I hear it. I've been working with jazz musician Charles Lloyd recently—we did an album together and we've done some shows together. And one of the songs he does, before I go out onstage, is a version of "Shenandoah"—and every time I hear it, it makes me cry. I don't know. I remember that song from when I was a child. It has one of those melodies that is just so beautiful, so gorgeous.

This is music that makes me cry. I can't imagine what it would be like to be lying in bed and know that you're dying. Hopefully I'm surrounded by loved ones. The way some people describe it . . . I guess if you're one hundred years old, you're pretty satisfied and ready to go. I feel like there's something greater than us, here and now. Somehow, somewhere. I grew up in the South and I've always been fascinated by the whole idea of good and evil, God and Satan, heaven and hell.

My faith these days? God is however you perceive it to be.

LUCINDA WILLIAMS

Lucinda Williams is a three-time Grammy Award–winning songwriter, often mixing blues and country with a unique southern gothic worldview. In 2017, Berklee College of Music awarded her an honorary doctorate in music.

I gave *Movies (and Other Things)* author Shea Serrano an impossible task: take ten iconic movie death scenes and choose better music for them. Here's what happened.

Movie Deaths (and Other Things)

BY SHEA SERRANO

FIRST, I WOULD LIKE TO SAY THAT ALL of these death scenes are perfectly scored. There was not one single entry on the list where, when I saw the death described here, I said, "Oh. I know. I know how to make this sadder." But here you go.

BLACK SWAN

NINA

I don't want you to give me a song here; I want you to give me one of those memory wipe things from *Men in Black*, because I saw this movie several years ago one time and have not watched it since, and I still have residual *Black Swan* Creeped Out-iness in my spine from it.

FORREST GUMP

JENNY

Give me "True Love Waits" by Radiohead here, but only if we can cut the scene so we get a long shot of Forrest next to Jenny's bed while she sleeps, or standing at her gravesite.

GET OUT

ROSE

Give me "I Hate U Bitch" by Z-Ro here, if for no other reason than because I suspect that Chris likely hated Rose a great deal in this moment.

THE GODFATHER: PART II

FREDO'S DEATH

Give me "24K Magic" by Bruno Mars here, but only because Fredo getting killed makes me really sad and this song makes me really happy. It's like that Jo line on that one episode of *The Office*: "I'm doing an opposites thing."

JAWS

THE SHARK

Give me "I Will Remember You" by Sarah McLachlan here, but you gotta have it set up so that we get some close-up slo-mo shots of Jaws like he's a dog in one of those adoption commercials they play on TV real late at night.

170

STAR WARS

DARTH VADER

Give me "It's Been Awhile" by Staind here (lol). As a pick, it doesn't make any sense at all, but the original *Star Wars* trilogy in my head has a very strong early-2000s vibe to it, because I didn't watch it until I was in college, so that's what's going on here.

THE LION KING

MUFASA

Give me "Wake Up" by Travis Scott. Technically, it doesn't really make sense here (the song is about not wanting to wake up), but you get the point. (Also, Travis talks about "pussy" in the song, which, if you squint, I mean . . . maybe a lion?)

PULP FICTION

VINCENT

Give me any unexpected song from any era in any genre here (there has to be at least one or two threads tying it to the moment, though), because that's the kind of thing that happens in a Quentin Tarantino movie.

DIE HARD

HANS GRUBER

Okay, this one is actually literally perfect and I'm not going to replace it with anything at all and you can go to hell for even asking me to, okay great thank you.

TITANIC

JACK

Give me "Ice Ice Baby" by Vanilla Ice here. I'm so sorry.

171

RICHARD REED PARRY

ARCADE FIRE

———

LAST SONG

"Small Hours"

BY JOHN MARTYN (1977)

I WOULD PICK THE SONG "SMALL HOURS" by John Martyn. Do you know that song? You should check it out. It's one of my top five recorded pieces of music of all time. It's probably my favorite on certain days, but it changes, depending on the day. It kinda sounds like the Holy Ghost in musical form. It's very unpremeditated in certain ways and a very incomplete song in certain ways. That's what I love about it. It's a song less in a Leonard Cohen literature kind of way and more in a musical creation way. It just feels like it's a few song lines . . . It's the beginning of a song that turns into a complete piece of music in a gentle way, one of the most unlabored things I've ever heard.

"Small Hours"

ARTIST
John Martyn

ALBUM
One World

LENGTH
8 minutes, 46 seconds

**WAS IT REALLY RECORDED
OUTSIDE, NEAR A LAKE?**
Yes! And here's what Phill Brown,
who recorded it, says about it now:
"I think the calm summer nights
and our approaching of blasting
John's guitar across the disused
gravel pit was pretty unique. My
memory is of hypnotic, floating,
opium-induced nights. "Small
Hours" was captured at four a.m.
It was magical then and to me still
is. I have it in my will to play it at
my funeral."

RICHARD
REED PARRY

Richard Reed Parry is a multi-instrumentalist member of Arcade
Fire. He also records and releases
music under his own name; his
latest solo albums, *Quiet River
of Dust Vol. 1 & 2*, are out on
ANTI- Records.

"Small Hours" was recorded outside, live. Martyn's a beautiful guitar player, and he's playing his guitar through an amplifier set up on a lake; the microphones are set up on the other side of the lake. And you can hear water and air in the background, and occasionally geese flying overhead. There's this beautiful space that's capturing nature without sounding like a nature recording. So it feels like music that was born out of earth, barely touched by the hand of man. That is such a sublime quality.

The nature of the song isn't very thought through. The structure of the song is very loose, very organic. The lyrics are very simple, yet personal and aspirational and small in a certain way. They're treated as everything for a moment. There's a big, gentle, benign, earthly sense around the whole thing.

So it's as much about a piece of music being born as a song that was written. It's more like an utterance than a piece of craft; though obviously, there's a lifetime of craft that went into his work. This feels effortless. Unconsidered in the most transcendent way.

I don't remember the first time I heard it, but I remember reading about it. I'm an obsessive nerd for the band Talk Talk, and the guy who recorded Talk Talk records—the really memorable ones—was involved in recording this song. I made a mental note when he described what he recorded of *Oooh, I'm going to like that!* It was on my "to-check-out" list, but I never did until I met my girl-friend-now-wife. She was a real big John Martyn fan and had a "Best of" that she used to listen to in her painting studio. I remember hearing it and thinking I could listen to that song on repeat forever. It doesn't have a beginning or an end; it just rolls along. I was immediately taken by it.

It's deeply peaceful and comforting. It's ashes to ashes, dust to dust in the most benign, unpainful kind of way. An all-is-right-in-the-world-and-this-too-shall-pass kind of way.

BETH ORTON

LAST SONG

"Suzanne"

BY LEONARD COHEN (1967)

I WAS THINKING ABOUT ALL THE PEOPLE I could have picked and all the songs I could have picked and decided it depends on how you would die. Will you die with your loved ones around you, and there's some nice gentle music on in the background? When my mum died, it was very important to her—she loved classical music, and we had her favorite music playing all the time, just easing her out from one place to the next.

BETH
ORTON

Over her twenty-five-year-plus career, British songwriter Beth Orton has released six albums under her own name and recorded with the Chemical Brothers, Beck, and Bert Jansch.

But really, it's connotation.

The first time I heard Leonard Cohen was when I was with my best friend, probably when I was fourteen. She was a raging alcoholic. We didn't know then that's what it was, but she ended up dying from it. It was pretty serious. She and I had so much fun. What was odd was that we would go out and have these wild nights together—and when we would come home, we would listen to Leonard Cohen. I had never heard music like that before. At fourteen, I was like, who is that man? That voice?

He's the ultimate father figure. The romanticized version of that man you go to for answers. I have no baggage attached to his music. "Suzanne"—it's an ultimate song. It's forgiveness, acceptance, tenderness. These parables and lullabies and poetry that he weaves into all his songs. And he lived his life through songwriting. He said he handed it over. And I was thinking, maybe I did that too.

Joni Mitchell helped me. Joni Mitchell is perfection. But at the same time, I'm not looking for perfection. I'd want the comfort of Leonard Cohen's voice. I'd want to be held by his mystery, his love, his romanticism. I could feel the safety of him, holding me into the next world, from one side to the next. It's not like a song I'd want to play at my funeral. It's not about me; it's not about being one of his characters. Because he sings so much about relationships and love in such a particular way and everything is tinged with nature, with religion. He digs to great depths. It seems like he handed his life over to this journey, wanting to discover his songwriting.

With that, he's Zen. And he made his work his pilgrimage. I hear that. He speaks of the lowest and the highest kind. He can make something simple and profound. But I was thinking about how harsh he could be at times, and how his compassion allows for that honesty. You know it comes from compassion. And you know he's speaking about himself as much as he's speaking about someone else.

177

"Suzanne"

ARTIST
Leonard Cohen

ALBUM
Songs of Leonard Cohen

LENGTH
3 minutes, 49 seconds

FIRST RECORDED BY
Judy Collins in 1966

BUT WHY?
Because it was first written as a poem and she got a hold of it and did it up.

IT'S ABOUT
A platonic relationship with a friend, Suzanne Verdal, who made him tea and fed him oranges. Fans have long been obsessed with the tea and oranges.

"Suzanne" speaks of love. And I think the most exciting parts of being alive are loving someone else and writing songs. And he's done so much, so well. A song like "Suzanne" doesn't trouble me with memories and correlate to a sadness. It just gives me hope. I hear that I will search for that love, whether I will find it or not. And he gave his life over to that as well. It's the search for what love means to him. That gives life great purpose.

Leonard Cohen has always dug into our mortality—he asked all the questions, and it's just extraordinary.

JIM JAMES

MY MORNING JACKET

———

LAST SONG

"*I Believe in You*"

BY TALK TALK (1988)

THE FIRST TIME I EVER THOUGHT ABOUT this whole death song thing, I was sitting around a campfire years ago with my friend Patrick. He always said he wanted us to play Led Zeppelin's "Ten Years Gone" at his funeral, and back then I thought it would probably also be the last song he would want to hear. What a beautiful song. If he happens to go before me, you bet I will play that fucking song so loud and so many times . . . over and over again. And he will hear it somewhere, smiling.

For a while I thought if I had to pick one song I would go with "In a Sentimental Mood" by Duke Ellington—but a very specific version, a vinyl copy that I have listened to so many times. The first time I ever heard it was actually with my same friend Patrick. He played it for us one night and I just couldn't believe it. This was grand architecture. This was the impossible music of true genius straight from the heavens brought to life down here on earth.

When I imagine hearing it as I die, I am inside the blood vessels of the Lord, whatever God is, I am in a grand Gothic cathedral made of God's blood and guts and sweat and tears. Brains and blood and piss and shit and cum. I am shooting down the cock of the universe with ten billion others into the great mother's vagina to be born again. I am a little baby fresh and new. I am a man. I am a woman. I am falling in love. I am dying again. I am a shooting star. I see all of my past lifetimes and get a little hint of the future. I can feel all of my failures, each and every one. And every time, I succeeded! *Ah, the glory and triumph!!!* I can see the birth of every child I ever had, screaming and crying, newborn in the arms of every woman I ever loved. I can feel myself giving birth. I can see all of the men I ever loved and all the beautiful scenes we shared . . . I can know love is this *giant* concept: bigger than "men" and "women," bigger than any race or creed—I see love as the great connector, the great source, the meaning of God so big and beautiful and boundless. It is the sound of God, a swirling whirling ball of penises and vaginas and lips and hips and breasts and arms and hearts and legs every size and color of the rainbow singing out to me . . . something I will never be able to even come close to understanding, but I *feel* it *so* powerfully. I can feel this love . . .

Then I get hit by a bus. Or I get shot. Or maybe the plane crashes. Or perhaps I take my own life.

Or maybe I just didn't get lucky—poor health . . . and down the tube I go . . . and now it's dark.

"In a Sentimental Mood" is playing from far off . . . I am drifting toward the sound in an old swan boat down a cracking tiled subway tunnel filled with water underneath the ground lit by golden vintage orange warm-colored LED candle bulbs flickering on the water. I am newly dead, freshly dead, deader than a fucking doornail—reminiscing on what I experienced in this life that just a moment ago came to a close . . . and looking forward to the next world, the next earth mother, the next womb I will enter to start it all over again, I am trying to remember it all before I forget again and pop out as the next Jim or Jim-ette or maybe I will be an eagle or an ant or a worm or a doggy. I take a box and some tissue and wrap them up—I leave some of these memories down there in the tunnel, hoping the next me will find them somehow, perhaps in a déjà vu, and that they may be of some use to the next me, whoever I am. *Oh shit*—if I can only tell the next me not to make this mistake or that misstep . . . or to make sure and really *love* every chance he gets—don't be scared! Don't be afraid to ask for help! You know . . . just little tips. Things that might help the next me.

But just then the tunnel comes to a fork and the boat starts to drift somewhere else I would have never guessed. And down this tunnel I hear Mark Hollis singing to me "I Believe in You." Oh, yes—I remember now, I was dying and this song was playing in my car when I fell asleep at the wheel and flew off the road . . . I remember now the rumble strips, the car smashing the guardrail and waking me up, the car hitting the water and all the noise and glass and the music I *just happened* to be listening to slowly getting drowned out . . . *Spirit of Eden* . . . It was late and I was tired and in a hurry and goddamn it, I was just trying to get

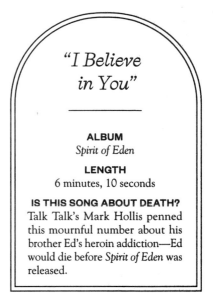

"*I Believe in You*"

ALBUM
Spirit of Eden

LENGTH
6 minutes, 10 seconds

IS THIS SONG ABOUT DEATH?
Talk Talk's Mark Hollis penned this mournful number about his brother Ed's heroin addiction—Ed would die before *Spirit of Eden* was released.

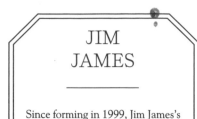

JIM
JAMES

Since forming in 1999, Jim James's My Morning Jacket has become one of the biggest rock bands of the past twenty years, headlining festivals and arenas. James is also a solo artist and a producer, working over the years with a wide range of artists, such as Booker T. Jones, Bright Eyes, and the Flaming Lips.

back home. And that was it. And now I am here drifting down the tunnel again . . . And I start to rise up out of the boat . . . I feel his hands underneath my arms . . . He is some kind of spirit angel pulling me up out of the boat and into the air . . . up through the subway tiles, up through the earth and into the clouds. I thought I knew what I wanted, I thought I knew, but I had no fucking idea. Everything changes. "Spirit. Spirit." He sings in my ear as he pushes me up into the stars to become a little worm, a little sperm, to shoot up and out and maybe take form, maybe meet the egg, maybe do it all again . . . if I'm lucky.

ONE LAST SONG: FINAL THOUGHTS

THE IDEA FOR THIS BOOK CAME TO ME ONE night after drinking a bit. I was waiting for New Jersey Transit to usher me out of Hoboken, coming home on a weeknight after staying out a bit too late to see a band I can't remember now. But I remember sitting there on the train, thinking about death, and thinking about what the last song I'd want to hear would be. And why it would always be "Terrapin Station" by the Grateful Dead. A song I found when I was seventeen, just learning about the band, a new relationship with an artist that would last decades. I was listening to it that night and heard something new, probably. I always hear something new with that one. I think that's why I like it so much.

But at that moment, I just thought it would be a good question to ask a bunch of musicians to see what they would say.

For the first couple of artists I interviewed for this, I led with the question: "So, what's the last song you'd want to hear before you died?" Killer Mike and A. C. Newman were good sports in that they didn't question why I was so morbid. But as I kept probing people for their last songs, it became clearer to me that this wasn't as simple a question as I had thought it was that night in Hoboken.

So I stopped asking people what they wanted to hear before they died and started asking people what they wanted to hear as their last song on earth. Just that rephrasing did wonders. It made the finality of the original question almost disappear. It acknowledged something deeper, too—that your time on earth may not be your last time existing, if you ascribe to such notions. It allowed for possibility.

But it also allowed for a softer, different type of thinking on something that's really hard for people. Thinking about letting go of music and songs—artistic creations we hold so dear to us, and that the people in this book hold dear to their livelihoods. That was probably the biggest "revelation" if there was one—that the attachment we have to music runs so deep, and is so ingrained into our essence, that when forced to narrow it down to a final thing, it becomes extremely difficult. Maybe even an exercise in futility, for some. But I also learned that people's connection to whatever song it may be is so different and so unique and so wrapped up in their personal story with their life on earth—it could never be the song you wanted to hear before you die. It had to be the song you wanted to hear when you leave.

Tell me your song. Tell me your story. I bet it's a good one.

AUTHOR'S NOTE

The artist chapters in this book were constructed from interviews I did from 2018 to 2020. They were edited for clarity and condensed for brevity.

The research for the chapters was culled from a variety of sources, and in some instances, there were conflicting reports about what really happened decades ago. I worked to verify everything as fact; but as with a lot of things in pop music, debate likely still exists.

SOURCES

PAGE 22

Hattenstone, Simon. "Interviewing Lou Reed: Not a Perfect Day." *The Guardian*, May 19, 2003. https://www.theguardian.com/music/2003/may/19/artsfeatures.popandrock

PAGE 27

Montgomery, James. "Katy Perry Reveals the Inspiration Behind 'Firework.'" MTV.com, November 9, 2010. http://www.mtv.com/news/1651895/katy-perry-reveals-inspiration-behind-firework/

PAGE 109

Leigh, Spencer, and Jon Kutner. *1,000 UK Number One Hits*. Omnibus Press, 2005.

PAGE 137

Rosen, Miss. "The Story Behind the Notorious B.I.G.'s spooky "Life After Death" Album Cover." *The Undefeated*, May 19, 2017. https://theundefeated.com/features/notorious-big-life-after-death-album-cover/

Marchese, David. "The SPIN Interview: Lou Reed." *SPIN*, November 2008. https://www.spin.com/2008/11/spin-interview-lou-reed/

Du Noyer, Paul. *Conversations with McCartney*. Hodder & Stoughton, 2015.

PAGE 159

Greenberg, James. "This Magic Moment." *DGA Quarterly*, Spring 2015.

PAGE 160

Wigler, Josh. "*Game of Thrones* Composer Breaks Down 7 Key Music Moments." *The Hollywood Reporter*, April 5, 2019. https://www.hollywoodreporter.com/live-feed/game-thrones-ramin-djawadi-score-explained-1199740

Fernandez, Maria Elena. "A Swan Song for *Lost* Composer Michael Giacchino." *Los Angeles Times*, May 13, 2010.

ACKNOWLEDGMENTS

PICKING A LAST SONG IS hard. Putting this all together wasn't easy either and benefited from a number of people's belief in this book and me.

First, my editor, Samantha Weiner (Bruce Springsteen, "Thunder Road"), was on board for this project from minute one and lobbied for its existence many times over. Not only that—she's a wonderful editor and person, and it's been a joy to work with her for more than two years on this. Sam, thank you.

I'm also indebted to all the artists in this book who lent their time and energy and thoughts to this question and the book's concept. Everyone took it very seriously, which reassured me very early on that I was on to something.

But I couldn't just text whomever I felt like and ask them what their one last song would be. This book also benefited from numerous managers and publicists who got this idea to the musicians and helped me schedule time with them. Thank you: Jennifer Farmer, Joe Goldberg, Jeremy Westby, Carolyne Klein, Terri Hinte, Grace Jones, Matt Hanks, Judy Silverman, Catherine Herrick, Mac Cregan,

Laura Bergstein, Dana Erickson, Kevin Kiley, Jessica Linker, Jacob Daneman, Patrick Tilley, Mary Moyer, Eufaula Garrett, Scott Booker, Derek Brown, Jim Flammia, Howard Greyolds, Kelly Kettering, Olivia Harrington, Eric Mayers, Darin Harmon, and Danny Kahn.

The team at Abrams is fantastic and have spent countless hours bringing this to life: Thank you, Diane Shaw (Nina Simone, "Here Comes the Sun"), Elizabeth Broussard (Priscilla Ahn, "Dream"), Lisa Silverman (Fleetwood Mac, "Gypsy"), Kristen Milford (Louis Armstrong, "La Vie En Rose"), Rachael Marks (Green Day, "Jesus of Suburbia"), Mamie Vanlangen (Matt Nathanson, "Little Victories"), Andrew Gibeley (Adele, "When We Were Young"), and Eli Mock (Animal Collective, "Banshee Beat"). Your work on this was critical.

The artists at Studio Muti in South Africa brought these stories to visual life in ways that I never imagined and that I utterly adore.

Big thanks to Jim James for taking the time not only to express a last song choice, but also to write a beautiful foreword.

Thank you to Shea Serrano (OutKast, "Elevators [Me and You]") for tweeting at me when I was at MTV many years ago and asking to write about Houston rappers for the website I was editing that no longer exists. And now, several years later, lending advice and also writing to this book. You're the best.

These people have heard me talk about this book for a long time at this point and provided valuable feedback on everything, from how bad my jokes were to the concept itself and everything in between. Jaime and Jon David (Cypress Hill, "I Ain't Going Out Like That"; Jonsi, "Happiness"), Adam Mandel (the Beatles, "I Will"), Mike Friedman (Joy Division, "Atmosphere"), Kristen Bahler (My Bloody Valentine, "Sometimes"), Jay Potter (Elliott Smith, "Waltz #2"), Matt Fine (Topaz Gang, "Sk8lyf"), Martin Zager (Cocteau Twins, "Bluebeard"), and Tyler Dickson (Sonic Youth, "Dirty Boots").

My fact-checking hero, Lauren Goldstein (the Beatles, "She Said She Said"), spent time going over things with a fine-toothed comb and thus allowed me to sleep at night. Also, shout out to Xander Zellner (the Band, "The Weight") and Trevor Anderson (Marvin Gaye, "Got to Give It Up") at *Billboard* for helping me with geeky chart queries.

Thank you to my family, especially my parents, Doug and Elaine, for your love and support over the years and for looking the other way when I was blowing off school or homework or some other responsibility to go watch bands play music.

While writing a book about death, I was fortunate to have two people in my life who were just getting started with theirs: my kids, Liam and Emma. I don't want to think about your last songs, so I'll just keep listening to all the Taylor Swift, Shakira, and *SportsCenter* broadcasts you continue to blast throughout the house.

Lastly, my wife, Diedre (Fleetwood Mac, "Landslide"), is a constant source of inspiration and love in ways that are impossible to quantify and articulate. Thank you, Diedre, for being by my side for so many years and believing in me. I don't want us to ever end.

Editor: Samantha Weiner
Designer: Eli Mock
Production Manager: Rachael Marks

Library of Congress Control Number: 2019939750
ISBN: 978-1-4197-3820-3
eISBN: 978-1-68335-804-6

Charts on pages 42–46 courtesy of
Co-Op Funeralcare 2019 Funeral Music Chart Study

Printed and bound in the United States

10 9 8 7 6 5 4 3 2 1

Abrams Image books are available at special discounts
when purchased in quantity for premiums and promotions
as well as fundraising or educational use. Special editions
can also be created to specification. For details, contact
specialsales@abramsbooks.com or the address below.

Abrams Image® is a registered trademark of Harry N.
Abrams, Inc.

ABRAMS The Art of Books
195 Broadway, New York, NY 10007
abramsbooks.com